MYSTERY
SHOPPING
MADE SIMPLE

MYSTERY
SHOPPING
MADE SIMPLE

DR. ILISHA S. NEWHOUSE

ILLUSTRATIONS BY JO ANNA LARSON

McGraw-Hill

New York Chicago San Francisco Lisbon London Madrid
Mexico City Milan New Delhi San Juan Seoul
Singapore Sydney Toronto

3 4 5 6 7 8 9 0   DOC/DOC   0 9 8 7 6 5 4

ISBN 0-07-144002-X

McGraw-Hill books are available at special quantity discounts to use as premiums and sales promotions, or for use in corporate training programs. For more information, please write to the Director of Special Sales, McGraw-Hill Professional, Two Penn Plaza, New York, NY 10011-2298. Or contact your local bookstore.

Caution: Do not purchase this book if you intend to mystery shop in Nevada or Florida. It is illegal to mystery shop in these states without a private investigators license. Additionally, the state of Florida only allows mystery shopping in the restaurant industry for customer service assignments.

This publication is designed to provide accurate and authoritative information in regard to the subject matter covered. It is sold with the understanding that neither the author nor the publisher is engaged in rendering legal, accounting, or other professional service. If legal advice or other expert assistance is required, the services of a competent professional person should be sought.
—From a Declaration of Principles jointly adopted by a Committee of the American Bar Association and a Committee of Publishers.

This book is printed on recycled, acid-free paper containing a minimum of 50% recycled, de-inked fiber.

This book is dedicated to the wonderful staff at South Mountain Community College and the City of Chandler Parks and Recreation, with special recognition to Debbie Nicholson, Stacey Ayers, and Michael Luketich. If not for your faith, trust, and support, this book would not have been possible.

To my son, Wesley, and my husband, Lee, you are my life, my world, my everything, and I love you.

CONTENTS

For updates and revisions, please visit www.newhouseservices.com.

A NOTE FROM NICCOLE ROGERS

National Center for Professional
   Mystery Shoppers & Merchandisers, Inc.
ncpms@ncpmscenter.org
www.ncpmscenter.org

September 1, 2003

Dear Friends:

It is an honor and a privilege to endorse this book. The data are organized, factual, and easy to follow. It truly is mystery shopping made simple.

This book can provide guidance to new and seasoned mystery shoppers. I cannot recall another publication that is as detailed and delivers the same level of information.

I know that you will enjoy reading and learning from this book.

Sincerely,
Niccole Rogers, M. A., President

ACKNOWLEDGMENTS

A very special thank you to Niccole Rogers, founder and president of the National Center of Professional Mystery Shoppers. Thank you so much for your guidance and support, and thank you for being a true hero as well as the backbone for mystery shoppers everywhere.

PREFACE

How I Discovered Mystery Shopping

I was working on my master's degree in organizational management while acting as human resource director for a private university. I was trying to be everything to everyone, and taking care of my son was just one more thing I had to do. So my husband and I decided that I should probably open my own business, but what? I started off with an errand service, and then a traveling notary service, but nothing came of either of those ventures. Then it hit me. I had a friend in California who used to mystery-shop for Mimi's Café. She would go to different restaurants for breakfast, lunch, and dinner, write a report, and get paid. I thought, I can do that, and I could bring my son with me, too!

I started to research the industry and received my first assignment a month later, in August 1997. It was a retail store, and it paid $8. From that moment I have acquired over 400 accounts and currently shop for about 200 different companies. This manual is a collection of almost 7 years of mystery-shopping research as well as 4 years of teaching a How to Be a Mystery Shopper course. I hope you find this information to be helpful. Mystery shopping will not make you rich; however, it will improve your quality of life and provide newfound freedom and an alternative to working within the corporate machine.

Author's Welcome

Welcome to the mystery-shopping industry. My name is Ilisha Newhouse, and I am the author of this book. This book will provide you
with a tutorial to the mystery-shopping industry. It will consist of a
brief history, descriptions, methods of getting started, and other
sources. In addition, you will get an explanation of report types and
average payment for each report. Finally, it will discuss tax issues and
provide tax forms, as well as providing helpful Internet links for future
tax and small business questions. However, this book will not provide
information on who shops whom. For example, it does not tell you
which mystery-shopping companies have the Ritz Carlton account, so
that you can contact them and mystery-shop the Ritz Carlton. This
information is not provided because it would violate confidentiality
agreements. Finally, this is not a job offer. Many students pick up my
book and attend my course expecting to receive a $50,000 a year job
that day. By no means am I offering you a job; however, I am offering
instructions on how to start a new career. After you have read the book
or completed the course, the decision as to how often you would like
to mystery-shop will be yours. Make no mistake, mystery shopping is
hard work, but it is the best job you will ever have. Personally, I would
rather sit around the pool at a four-star resort typing up reports on my
laptop than be stuck in an office cubicle being yelled at by some fool
who is upset because I am 2 minutes late. Whether you decide to dine
for the reimbursements, shop part-time as a stay-at-home mom with
your children, supplement your income as a senior citizen, or grab the
bull by the horns and shop full-time, I wish you well with your ventures. This book is a valuable resource for your newfound career.

Blessings,
Dr. Ilisha Newhouse

INTRODUCTION

Is This for Real?

This is one of the most frequent questions I receive when I state what I do for a living. Many people are flabbergasted by the opportunity and the size of the industry. Mystery shopping is an industry with more than 750 companies in the continental United States alone and opportunity to travel overseas. It is a respected industry with organizations for continuity, ethics, and support. In addition, mystery shoppers are utilized by almost every type of business you can imagine from gas stations to grocery stores to hotels. Finally, anyone can start mystery shopping with an investment of zero, for you will be doing things you would be doing anyway, such as going to the grocery store or putting gas into your car!

A Typical Day As a Shopper

My niche is fine dining and luxury hotels. A typical hotel assignment consists of tipping and utilizing the valet, the bellboy, room service, and the day spa. The corporations that contract mystery shoppers want shoppers to utilize all the amenities, the restaurants, and features of the hotel. So mystery shoppers may be asked to visit all the bars, restaurants, gift shops, and beauty salons in the hotel. A typical hotel day for me would be to use the valet and have the bellhop escort me to my room. I then call for a massage appointment at the day spa, change my clothes, and visit the bar at the pool. I begin typing my report on my laptop at the pool as I observe the exterior cleanliness of the hotel, pool, and tennis court or playground. I stroll to my massage appointment, then go back to my room for a nap to test the wake-up call or alarm system. I make reservations for dinner at one hotel restaurant and for breakfast at the other hotel restaurant. I visit the bar in the atrium for a before-dinner drink and then stroll to the five-star restaurant for steak and lobster. When I leave the restaurant, I wander into the upbeat nightclub for a chat with the DJ and the bartender. Maybe I'll dance or maybe not. I head up to my room and bump into the maid, who greets me and inquires about my stay. I ask for additional towels, and she brings them to me 2 minutes after I arrive in the room. Oh, a lightbulb is out! I call maintenance immediately, and they promptly change the bulb, with an apology and a $5 certificate for room service. Oh, yes! I must call room service for some strawberries and champagne.

The room service associate arrives within minutes of my placing the order, and the expeditor is graciously tipped for his promptness. I spend a couple of hours writing a narrative of my experiences: the atmosphere, the service, and the food. It is morning, and I take a long hot shower before breakfast. I have a fine breakfast; however, I purposely forgot my room key to check for proper security procedures. The front desk clerk is very accommodating and follows procedure by asking for identification. While I am at the front desk, I ask for a late checkout and receive no resistance to my request. I return to my room and finish typing my report up to the point of checkout. I pack my bag and check out at the front desk. The bellhop retrieves my bag, and my car is retrieved by the valet. Both are prompt and friendly, and thus receive gracious tips. I return home and finish writing my report on my computer. I email it to the contracting agency and announce out loud how wonderful it is to be paid to be the princess! My total reimbursed expenses are typically $1,000 per night, and I receive a fee of $500. Yes, it is good to be the princess.

Testimonials

In July 2001, I saw an article in the *Ahwatukee Foothills News* regarding a mystery-shopping course. The headline intrigued me, since I had worked in the retail industry previously and had been shopped by a shopping service on many occasions. The article went on to say that

Dr. Ilisha Newhouse was teaching this course at the local community college branch in my area. I tried to sign up for the course but was told that there was a waiting list and I would be notified when there was another class. I actually took the course in October of the same year.

Dr. Newhouse presented a 3-hour-long class based on her personal shopping experiences, insights, and knowledge. She presented the course in a clear, concise, easy-to-understand manner. Ilisha discussed the how, what, why, when, and where of mystery shopping and merchandising. She provided excellent handouts that contained the names, telephone numbers, and email addresses of mystery-shopping companies. She discussed tax considerations and the letter of intent, or industry-specific résumé, and gave us ideas on how to evaluate a client's business and how to write a report.

As I mentioned above, I took the course in October 2001. I signed up with a lot of shopping companies; I was assigned my first shop in December 2001. I was getting a little frustrated, and Ilisha offered an advanced course in mystery shopping in January 2002. The second course helped me immensely in writing a letter of intent. I hit the street running February 1, 2002. I currently have maintained my full-time position and have shopped part-time as a hobby. Just by shopping part-time in evenings and weekends, I have had shops totaling in excess of $3,500 through August 30, 2002. That's an extra $500 to $600 a month for dining out, visiting apartments, and grocery shopping! I work on referral only now. I have seen other mystery-shopping books and course materials available for hundreds of dollars. Ilisha's book, course, and materials are well worth the money invested in this business. She is always available to answer questions and offer advice. She is the owner of a leads list for shoppers in Arizona.

The bottom line is that here is an opportunity to do what you want to do, get paid for it, and enhance your quality of life. I conduct my shopping assessments in the late afternoon and weekends. Everyone has a niche; I found my niche in apartment shopping. Reach out, grab for Ilisha's brass ring! You will not be sorry. I owe my successes to Dr. Ilisha Newhouse and her courses, materials, and insights. She has a tremendous amount of experience in this area of small business.

Sincerely,
D. Metcalf

✳ ✳ ✳

I quit my 60+-hour/week job as an IT manager in March 2002. I was burned out. I had been mystery shopping on the side since 1989, but I had been turning down assignments because I didn't have time for them on top of my job and family responsibilities.

My kids were acting up, my grandmother needed more help, and I knew I needed to change my lifestyle so I could be there for my family when it counted. In a year or two grandma could be gone, and my kids wouldn't have time for me!

I have recently added online teaching and merchandising to my repertoire. In addition, I am on salary to a local real estate developer, and I occasionally help out with IT projects at former places of employment, but as an independent contractor.

I earn about half of what I did as an IT manager for a nonprofit organization, and I work 10 to 30 hours most weeks.

Heidi Titchenal

Ms. Heidi
Certified Online Instructor
NCPMS Learning Center
heidi@ncpmscenter.org
Visit the Learning Center

✳ ✳ ✳

I attended Dr. Ilisha Newhouse's mystery-shopping class in July of 2003. After attending the first session, I obtained an assignment. I completed my first shop before the second class had commenced. The first edition of her book, *Mystery Shopping Made Simple,* was an enormous help in guiding me through the ins and outs of how to enter the realm of mystery shopping.

I have since completed the four-session course with Dr. Newhouse. Her expertise has been invaluable in finding available shops and companies that are seeking new shoppers in the current market. I was pleasantly surprised by the ease with which I was able to acquire my first assignment. My initial shop was an apartment evaluation yielding me $40. I have since joined several mystery-shopping companies, and my choice of jobs has been quite diverse. My gross income for the first month was $430. For the upcoming month, I have scheduled over six assignments thus far.

Dr. Newhouse's insight into the mystery-shopping world has given me the knowledge I needed to establish a business of my own. Without her expertise, I would not have known how to set up the various financial accounts necessary to track and report my business activities. Her knowledge has been essential in my quest to be successfully self-employed.

Time and time again I find myself referring to her book for various tips on how to improve my technique while continuing to grow in this ever-expanding business venture. I would highly recommend her book and class to anyone interested in learning how to establish a successful mystery-shopping business from home.

E. Reeds

Commonly Asked Questions—Quick Facts

The Top 10 Mystery-Shopping Questions

1. *How do I get started?* It is very easy to become a full-time mystery shopper. However, you must first educate yourself about the industry and then decide whether mystery shopping is a match for you. You should not enter this industry without awareness of scams and business law. You can acquire all the knowledge you need by reading this book, taking a class, or researching the subject on the Internet. See Chapters 1 to 14.

2. *Do I really need certification?* Certification is an option. You do not need to become certified in order to become a mystery shopper. However, everyone can benefit from the acquisition of additional knowledge. See Chapter 13.

3. *How can I find a list of mystery-shopping companies?* See Chapter 4.

4. *Is this for real?* The mystery-shopping industry has been around since the 1940s and its annual net is around $600 million.

5. *Can I really make money mystery shopping?* A full-time shopper can make around $40,000 per year. See Chapter 1.

6. *How do I find jobs?* You must first educate yourself about the industry, compose a letter of intent, and make contact. See Chapter 4.

7. *What is mystery shopping?* Mystery shopping is the act of posing as a customer anonymously and evaluating an establishment for a fee. See Chapter 1.

8. *Should I pay to be listed?* An information list is another option. See Chapter 4.

9. *How do I find out what company mystery-shops my favorite store?* You can narrow your search to the specific industry. However, it violates confidentiality agreements to ask publicly which company mystery-shops a specific entity. See Chapter 4.

10. *Can I take my kids on my assignments?* Generally, you may take your children on your assignments. However, there are rare occasions, such as fine dining assignments, when they ask that you do not bring small children.

Industry Overview

Over 750 companies provide mystery-shopping services. Income is estimated to be $400 to $600 million annually.

The actual industry income is unclear because different types of firms offer mystery-shopping services (e.g., retailers themselves, mystery-shopping providers, market research firms), and they are sometimes offered as a bundled package with other business services. However, a shopper can make around $40,000 full-time or $20,000 part-time with the proper effort.

Why Companies Use the Feedback and Comments from Mystery Shoppers

- Determine the effectiveness of training
- Gauge employee knowledge and morale
- Review business procedures and policies
- Measure organization performance
- Understand how customers view their business

Four Top Markets Using Mystery Shoppers and Average Pay

- Restaurants (free meal to $150 fee plus reimbursements)
- Retail ($12 to $60)
- Banking/financial institutions ($30 to $70)
- Hotels (reimbursements only to $4,000 plus reimbursements)

Laws

- Nevada and Florida have laws on the books regarding mystery shopping. Nevada's law states that all mystery shoppers must hold a private investigator's license.

- You must pay social security if you net over $400, and you must pay state and federal tax if you net over $600.

- You must report every penny you make as a shopper, even if you operate at a loss.

Certification

The industry adopted certification in January 2003. Over the next 5 years, it is estimated that 80 percent of all mystery shoppers will become certified.

Quick Facts

- Eighty percent of mystery shoppers are paid 4 to 8 weeks after an assignment is completed.

- Seventy percent of mystery shoppers are usually paid for additional travel expenses.

- Sixty percent of new mystery shoppers quit after 7 months.

- Seventy-nine percent of mystery shoppers have another full- or part-time job.

- Mystery shoppers most frequently evaluate restaurants, retail stores, hotels, and banking/financial institutions.

Statistics

The National Center for Professional Mystery Shoppers & Merchandisers (NCPMS) routinely gathers data from independent contractors to track trends in the industry. Here is a summary of the latest secret shopping (SS) data.

Sex

89 percent women

11 percent men

Age

42 percent are between the ages of 32 and 42

Highest Education Level

28 percent high school

23 percent undergraduate 4-year degree

12 percent graduate degree

Race

85 percent Caucasian

8 percent African American

3 percent Hispanic

Successful Skills of Mystery Shoppers

1. An eye for detail
2. A great memory
3. Patience
4. Ability to keep confidential information secure
5. Outstanding written and oral communication skills
6. Excellent time management
7. Ability to be self-motivated
8. Conflict resolution experience
9. Ability to meet deadlines
10. Ability to follow directions with ease
11. YOU MUST LOVE TO SHOP!

Things Mystery Shoppers Should Know

1. Mystery shopping is fun—but it is work.
2. On average, it takes mystery shoppers 60 days to collect payment for their work.
3. Mystery shoppers are usually considered independent contractors.
4. Despite rumors, mystery shoppers do not get a ton of "free stuff." They are usually paid a flat fee plus a small allowance.

5. Mystery shopping in medium and large cities is highly competitive.

Avoiding Scams

Often mystery shoppers are tricked into buying a list of companies. Most of this information is readily available on the Internet. The NCPMS also has a great list of links. A rule of thumb is, *"If it costs money, it is probably a scam."*

Articles

MS: Is a "mystery shopper" lurking...(2001)
http://www.ncpmscenter.org/forum/viewtopic.php?t=104

MS: Corporate Spies (2002)
http://www.ncpmscenter.org/forum/viewtopic.php?t=161

MS: Spy Game (2002)
http://www.ncpmscenter.org/forum/viewtopic.php?t=162

MS: Seller Beware (2001)
http://www.ncpmscenter.org/forum/viewtopic.php?t=163

MS: Spies in the Aisles (2002)
http://www.ncpmscenter.org/forum/viewtopic.php?t=164

MS: Secret Services
http://www.ncpmscenter.org/forum/viewtopic.php?t=179

MS: A Different View of Mystery Shopping
http://www.ncpmscenter.org/forum/viewtopic.php?t=189

MS: Interested in becoming a mystery shopper?
http://www.ncpmscenter.org/forum/viewtopic.php?t=193

Secret Shoppers Help Businesses
http://augustachronicle.com/stories/020700/abc_secret.shtml

The Key to More Customers, More Sales and More Profits
http://www.measure-x.com/tips/key%20to%20more%20
customers,%20more%20sales,%20and%20more%20profits.html

OTS Tests "Mystery Shopping" to Help Check Thrifts' Fair Lending Compliance
http://www.ots.treas.gov/docs/77065.html

How One Entrepreneur Lives Large—for Free–The Wall Street
   Journal Online
   http://www.startupjournal.com/ideas/services/20030611-
   frank.html

About NCPMS

The National Center for Professional Mystery Shoppers & Merchandisers (NCPMS) was started in 1999. It is the preferred online training
center for mystery shoppers. It is also has the biggest minority database. The NCPMS serves 40,000 companies, mystery shoppers, merchandisers, and schedulers annually. The NCPMS also trains
approximately 500 mystery shoppers online annually.

NCPMS Contact Information

National web site: www.justshop.org

Education center: www.ncpmscenter.org

Contact email: niccole@ncpmscenter.org

The president is Niccole Rogers. NCPMS prefers contact via email.

MYSTERY
SHOPPING
MADE SIMPLE

CHAPTER 1

What Is Mystery Shopping?

M ystery shoppers are also known as secret shoppers, service evaluators, consumer researchers, customer service researchers, auditors,
scouts, or market research/evaluators. A person who is new to the
industry is called a "Newbie." Mystery shopping is the anonymous act of
posing as an ordinary customer and evaluating a situation for a fee and/or
reimbursement for products or services purchased. You will receive thorough training and a questionnaire before you enter any location. You will
never walk into a facility not knowing what you are supposed to do or
what you are supposed to evaluate. In addition, you will not reveal your
identity as a mystery shopper during the evaluation, and you will not
include your identity anywhere in the report. The options in mystery
shopping are endless—from getting a car tuned up to spending the night
in a four-star hotel.

Who Would Make a Good Shopper?

Any living person can be a mystery shopper. Shoppers are needed in
all areas, from orthopedic shoes, to bars, to cruise lines. However,
remember that mystery shopping is a job, and therefore you must have
several qualities to be successful. Mystery shopping is not a match for
everyone. You must have an eye for detail, a great memory, patience,
the ability to keep confidential information secure, outstanding written and oral communication skills, excellent time management, the
ability to be self-motivated, conflict resolution experience, the ability

to meet deadlines, and the ability to follow directions with ease. Finally, *you must love to shop*!

Opportunities

Mystery shopping is done in every industry possible, and the opportunities are endless. The following is a list of potential opportunities:

Retail	Coffee shops	Apartments
Hardware	Wholesale clubs	Airports
Clothing	Bridal shops	Hotels
Boat supply	Car rentals	Auto parts stores
Fast food	Theaters	Tire stores
Fine dining	Grocery stores	Fine jewelry
Cruise lines	Drug stores	Outdoor Equipment Camping
Resorts	Pizza delivery/pick-up	Pizza reward mystery shops
Banks	Pet stores	
Cell phone stores	Carpet cleaners	
Gas stations	Casinos	

History of Mystery Shopping

Mystery shopping started back in the 1940s with financial institutions. A shopper would enter the banking establishment, make a cash deposit, and state that a receipt was not needed. Observations of how the transaction was processed or not processed were made. This type of assignment is called an integrity assignment and mainly deals with the potential act of theft.

From this type of assignment, mystery shopping has developed into a rather large and unique industry covering areas from auto repair to fast food. Just about every national chain establishment in your neighborhood is mystery-shopped monthly or weekly. In fact, some fast-food restaurants are mystery-shopped three times a day and shoppers are rotated. So this week, try to notice every chain establishment:

hotels, gas stations, grocery stores, video stores, apartments, and so on, not to mention every store in the local mall!

Who Wants This Service?

The institutions that want this service are corporations, franchises, owners, competition, and distributors. In this section I like to use the examples of a Burger King and a McDonald's. Both have corporations, franchises, owners, competition, and distributors.

Corporations

The corporate structure that operates your local corporate-owned McDonald's is very detached from the day-to-day operations and may frequently send shoppers to these locations to report activity. Additionally, if there is a complaint, such as about a dirty rest room, the corporation may send a shopper to a specific location to look into the complaint (in this case, examine the rest room).

Franchises

Both McDonald's and Burger King are franchises, and the franchisees have agreed to adhere to certain standards and utilize certain products. For example, we may be asked to evaluate the wrapping supplies to be certain that they are Burger King's and not purchased from a generic outside vendor. Additionally, we may be asked to count the number of pickles on a Big Mac or to weigh the actual meat of the burger.

Owners

The franchises have individual owners who may be having issues with individual employees or cleanliness. We may be asked to check for theft or to evaluate the cleanliness of a facility.

Competition

In this case, the Burger King may have two lines running out the door, whereas the McDonald's is like a ghost town. The owner of the McDonald's may ask us to visit the Burger King to see what exactly is occurring at the establishment or to purchase some products so that the ingredients may be examined.

Distributors

Finally, we may be asked to visit a location in order to view a particular product that the establishment has contracted to display, such as a happy meal toy or a video.

Contact

The above institutions will not be the contacting agent. Rather, a market research company or a mystery-shopping company will contact you. The institutions will contract with the research company or mystery-shopping company to perform the research and compile the data. You will be a third-party contractor and will be completely anonymous to the institution. Additionally, the research companies may contact a person called a scheduler to do the actual scheduling of shoppers for individual assignments. For example, Linda may call you at home and state that she is a scheduler for Flower Scheduling and is assigning a contract for ABC Associates to complete Bank of America assignments. An institution such as Bank of America will never contact you; only a shopping agency or a scheduler will contact you.

CHAPTER 2

Types of Assignments

There are many different types of assignments; however, most of them fit into five categories: integrity, purchase and return, quality control, customer service, or a combination of all of these.

Integrity

We discussed integrity assignments in Chapter 1 when we covered the history of mystery shopping. Most integrity assignments require two people. For example, one person will purchase an item in a convenience store, place a dollar on the counter, and walk out. The second person will observe what the employee does with the funds. He will also make another purchase and ask for a receipt as proof of his having been at the location. These types of assignments pay about $20 per person and are very easy to complete.

Another type of integrity assignment involves alcohol and tobacco purchases. If you have a child, grandchild, or sibling who is not of age, this type of assignment could be for you. The underage person makes the purchase, and the person who is of age notes the details of the transaction.

It is important to note that this type of assignment may require you to fill out a form stating that you will appear in a court of law should a lawsuit occur. This type of assignment is specifically designed to check for theft or illegal activity, and employees may be fired because of it. For this reason, you may be asked to appear. Most companies will compensate you at a rate of approximately $50 per hour for appearing as a witness.

Finally, note that this type of assignment is not for everyone. On one occasion when I was participating in an integrity shop, I was asked to confuse the convenience store clerk. Mind you, these employees are working double shifts at minimum wage, and most did not graduate from high school. I recall store clerks who stated that they could not smile and count at the same time because it was too hard. I felt very uncomfortable confusing these clerks in order to test their integrity, and I no longer feel that this type of assignment is compatible with my level of ethics.

Purchase and Return

You will be asked to enter an establishment and purchase an item, then return the item at a designated time, which is usually between 20 minutes and 2 months later. In this assignment you will evaluate the return process, professionalism, and procedures. You will note if the employee filled out the proper forms and if he or she was kind to you during the return process.

I recall one occasion when I was asked to visit a sock store that was about the same size as my kitchen. Not only was I to spend 20 minutes searching for the perfect pair of socks. I was then to return them within 30 minutes of purchasing them. The look on the salesperson's face was one to die for, especially after helping me find the perfect pair of socks and then having to process the return less than half an hour later! Not all purchase and returns are as funny as this one, but be sure to check the instructions to see if they are this funny.

I was also lucky enough to do a purchase and return of a high-end automobile. I went through the entire purchase process, with test drive included, and then got to utilize the vehicle overnight. It had a sunroof, and let's say I should have gotten a speeding ticket! I enjoyed the vehicle overnight and then returned it the next day, stating that I was a shopper and to please tear up the contract.

Quality Control

Quality control consists of noting the establishment's adherence to a defined quality standard. Examples are the preparation of a steak as desired and counting the number of pickles on a Big Mac. Additionally, the quality can involve the presentation of a product or the production of a product. For example, a soda may be wet on the outside of the cup or filled to the top with ice.

One time, I was asked to count the number of asparagus tips served to me and then to note how many were long and how many were short. Not all assignments are this detailed, but companies do want to know if you received everything you ordered and if it was prepared as you requested.

Customer Service

When you go to a store, the presentation should be such that it would merit future patronage and a recommendation to family and friends. The associate should greet you with a warm hello, ask questions to qualify your needs, and go to extremes to satisfy those needs, whether what you are purchasing is an oil change or a blouse. You should feel important, and the service should be attentive.

In reality, when you enter an establishment and ask, "Where are the tank tops?" the associate usually points, ignores you, or walks away singing. What associates are supposed to do is make you feel so important and respected that you want to tell all your friends and family about the store. So a typical scenario should be this: The associate greets you when you enter the store, asks how she can help you, tells you her name, asks for your name, and guides you to the proper area, pointing out different styles and colors as well as shorts, pants, or other accessories. She then should escort you to the dressing room and check on you frequently, as well as providing additional clothing in your size that she thinks you would be interested in. After you leave the dressing room, she should ask for the sale by asking, "Have you decided?" or "Are you ready to check out?" Next, she should escort you to the register and point out a current sale on accessories, such as earrings, belts, or stocking. Finally, she should ask if you would like to put the purchase on your department store credit card, and if you don't have one, she can open an account for you today and give you an additional 10 percent discount. The transaction should be processed promptly and accurately, and your clothing should be folded nicely. The associate should hand you your item, thank you for shopping at the store, wish you a wonderful day, and invite you to return real soon.

This is the type of treatment you should be receiving. When you are a shopper, not only do you learn how you are supposed to be treated, but you demand nothing less.

Product Check

The product check is by far one of the most exciting assignments. You will be asked to visit an establishment and note whether a certain product was displayed and presented. For example, you may be asked to visit a jewelry store and note whether the salesperson attempts to sell you a Sony watch. If the salesperson does so, you will offer him a prize, such as a gift certificate or a scratch card. I had an experience in which a sales associate suggested the correct item, and I handed her a scratch card. Well! She won a free trip to Hawaii, and I felt like Santa Claus! This is by far one of my favorite types of assignments to complete.

Assignment Types

Integrity

Purchase and return

Quality control

Customer service

Product check—rewards

CHAPTER 3

Getting Started

There are many ways to acquire assignments and you must decide which is best for you. These methods are computer access, phone, snail mail (U.S. Postal Service), fax, and email. Regardless of which method you utilize, you must first compose a letter of intent to organize your information and present yourself as a professional.

The Letter of Intent (LOIS)

The main purpose of a letter of intent (LOIS) is to save you time! Just about every company you apply to will ask the same questions, and it is a waste of time to write the same answer over and over again. The alternative is to compose an industry-specific résumé called a "LOIS." (This document is named after my mother, Lois Gonchar, and there is no significance to the *s* in Lois other than to honor her as being a fantastic person.)

The most common question I receive from my students is, "Do I really have to write a LOIS?" My answer is yes. To be honest, this is one of the most frustrating questions to receive from my students, for as a teacher, I want my students to succeed, but if the students are not organized and focused, they will certainly fail. So my advice is: If you want to appear organized and focused as a professional shopper, you will compose a LOIS. I wish there were an easier solution; however, I found the composition of a LOIS to be the best shortcut to acquiring contracts rapidly. Please do not see the LOIS as a roadblock; instead, see it as a shortcut to success.

The main sections of a LOIS are the introduction, your shopping experience, why you think companies need this service, your best shopping experience, your worst shopping experience, places where you travel frequently and periodically, and a nice conclusion. It should be approximately four to five paragraphs in length, one page, and it should contain all of your contact information, such as your fax, phone, address, email address, and, of course, your name.

Upon completion of the LOIS, you will find communicating your intentions via email, fax, snail mail, or online to be extremely easy. You will simply send the letter via fax or snail mail, copy and paste it online, or attach it as a document via email. Whatever your choice of contact method may be, the composition of a LOIS will shorten your journey as well as provide a bold statement of professionalism.

Letter of Intent (LOIS)

- Introduction—education, job history, skills, dependability, and so on
- Why you think companies need this service
- Your best shopping experience
- Your worst shopping experience
- Areas where you travel frequently and periodically
- Closing statement and contact information
- Continuous revisions to include new experience

Writing the LOIS

Writing the LOIS can be slightly intimidating, so I have broken the following section into six easy parts to assist you with the composition of your personal LOIS. Each part will include an explanation, a sample of content, and space for jotting down your own personal criteria. I have provided samples of several LOISs as a source to get you started. Please take your time in this area, for your letter of intent is a representation of who you are and what your writing style is to the organizations from which you desire assignments.

1. The Introduction

The introduction of your letter is by far the most important part of the document. It should be bold, clear, and professional as well as appealing to the reader, prompting the desire to continue reading the document. The introduction should have such items as your name, a brief summary of your work experience with specific industries, and desirable skills.

For example:

> To Whom It May Concern:
> My name is Kathy Joe Lee, and I am an experienced shopper who would be a great asset to your organization. I have worked for 15 years as a human resource director, and I am great with people. In addition, I am detail-oriented, and organized, and I can act as an impartial observer with ease. If you are looking for someone with great communication and writing skills who is also a dependable and organized contractor, then look no further.

Introduction

_____

_____

_____

_____

2. Why Companies Need This Service

In order to succeed as a shopper, you need to understand why this service is offered and how a company can benefit from it. In this section, you will describe how companies can benefit in terms of improving quality, service, and cleanliness, which would lead to increased sales and regular customers.

For example:

> A good company will gain footage in the marketplace by examining cleanliness, quality control, and customer service on a regular basis. This in turn will show its appreciation of customers as well as employees and will ultimately result in an increased percentage of the marketplace, consumer loyalty, and employee satisfaction.

Why companies need this service

_____

_____

_____

_____

3. Best and/or Worst Shopping Experience

I know this category seems a little odd at first; however, many companies ask for a one-paragraph narrative covering your worst and/or best shopping experiences. They do this for a couple of reasons. First, this allows them to evaluate your ability to write clearly, in terms of putting two sentences together with correct grammar and also in terms of communicating what happened during an event. Second, they will note whether you can leave your feelings and emotions aside and communicate clear facts. Sometimes a shopper will have an extremely negative event, and he or she must remain unbiased by any other factors such as grooming, cleanliness, and stocking. In addition, you may write of a negative event that became positive once the opportunity to rectify the situation was offered. For example, you are offered an upgrade to a better room or a free meal with expensive wine. Finally, you should include the good experience in your LOIS and hold the poor experience in another file. This will make the letter a little more positive; however, at some point you will be asked to write about a poor shopping experience. If you write about this experience in advance, you will be prepared when the time occurs.

For example:

> The best customer service experience I have ever had was with the Saturn Company. Unfortunately, my battery died on a trip back from California. I called the 800 number for Saturn, and a tow truck was sent within an hour. I was then stuck in a small town called Yuma. Saturn paid for lunch for my family while our vehicle was being repaired, filled up our car with gas, and picked us up at the restaurant when the car was ready. This is only one of the wonderful experiences I have had with the Saturn Company, and because of its exceptional customer service, our next car will be a Saturn.

Best and/or worst shopping experience

_____

_____

4. Areas Where You Travel Frequently and Periodically

This is important because it tells the contracting companies what areas you are willing to visit on a regular basis and also what areas you visit periodically. If you have a relative in California or New York, you can possibly get a hotel assignment or a fine dining assignment while you are visiting. Another benefit is that if you complete one assignment during your visit, it is now a business trip, and you can write off such things such as airfare and car rental for 2 days as business expenses. This subject will be discussed further in Chapter 8.

For example:

I am located in a suburb 5 miles south of Phoenix. The cities I am available to shop in consist of, but are not limited to, Ahwatukee, Tempe, Chandler, Mesa, and Phoenix. In addition, I periodically visit Brooklyn, New York, and San Diego, California.

Areas of frequent and periodic travel

_____

_____

_____

_____

Companies may ask for zip codes in which you are available to travel. You may want to visit a free zip codes search engine, such as http://melissadata.com/ or www.usps.gov.

5. Closing Statement

Your closing statement is another chance to present yourself as an intelligent and motivated professional person. Close with something forward, pleasant, and bold that will make you stand out and promote the desire to contact you. You may also list your contact information, such as your name, address, phone number, fax number, email address, and so on, at the bottom of the letter, along with your signature.

For example:

I am looking forward to establishing a business relationship with you in the near future. Please feel free to contact me anytime. Thank you, and have a nice day!

Closing

_____

_____

_____

_____

_____

6. Mystery Shopping Experience

Once you begin receiving assignments, you are going to need to update your letter to promote your experience, which should lead to additional assignments. Some companies desire experience and some do not; nonetheless, it is important to honk your own horn and be proud of your experience as a seasoned shopper. This area should be placed in the LOIS between the introduction and why you think companies need this service.

For example:

I have worked as a mystery shopper for over 30 market researching companies during the last 4 years, and I have received assignments consisting of, but not limited to, evaluating department stores, restaurants (fine dining to fast food), hotels, motels, banks, mortgage lenders, insurance agencies, new home construction, mobile home centers, RV dealerships, bowling alleys, gas stations, motorcycle dealerships, apartments, grocery stores, car dealerships, automotive supply stores, and toy stores. These evaluations have included customer service, atmosphere, cleanliness, professionalism, visualization, time standards, management behavior, legal compliance, integrity, product quality, and overall ratings of the assignment. In addition, I have surveyed demographics and initiated exit interviews.

Mystery shopping experience

_____

_____

_____

_____

_____

Samples of LOIS

Selma Lopez
123 Bethany Home Rd
Phoenix, AZ 85040
(480) 940-7700
selmal@msn.com

My name is Selma Green, and I am a native resident of the city of Phoenix, Arizona. I have my Bachelor's Degree in Marketing from Arizona State University and my Master's Degree in Organizational Management from the University of Phoenix. Prior to starting my own home-based marketing business and becoming a stay-at-home mom, I was the chief executive of finance for an information technology company here in Phoenix. Prior to that, I was an assistant controller for a computer distributor at the franchise level. I have also been a karate instructor for the past 15 years with various gyms throughout the Phoenix metropolitan area.

Because I currently work at home, operating my marketing business and caring for my child, I have been able to develop several skills that I believe will prove beneficial to the shopping world. I am extremely organized and proficient in completing work in a timely manner. I have excellent attention to detail, and I have proved to be reliable in timely and urgent situations. With my marketing background, I have been exposed to various types of confidential information. I have audited several large corporations' data, ranging from financial information to databases. This line of work has required that I maintain the highest integrity and professionalism with all of my clients.

I believe that in today's economy, companies need to use mystery-shopping services to maintain a competitive advantage. Customer service and quality assurance are extremely important to today's consumers. I enjoy shopping and would welcome the opportunity to help improve the standards that today's companies should strive for.

My best shopping experience to date has been with my local pharmacist. My daughter has a chronic illness and requires several different medications on a daily basis. My pharmacist has made it his business to know my family by name, to contact us when he knows we may be needing refills, to contact my daughter's doctor when our prescriptions have expired, and to keep in contact with our insurance companies on any pertinent changes. My worst shopping experience was shopping for professional work clothes a few years ago when I was still employed outside of the home. I am Hispanic, and I am approximately 5 feet tall.

After choosing several outfits to purchase, I was overlooked by the salespeople because I didn't look "old enough" to be a professional.

Phoenix has many suburbs that I would be available to take assignments in. I frequently travel into areas such as Chandler, Tempe, Mesa, Ahwatukee, Gilbert, Apache Junction, Scottsdale, Fountain Hills, Glendale, Peoria, and Sun City. I periodically travel to the northern part of the state to Sedona, Flagstaff, Show Low, and Kingman. We also vacation in Reno and South Lake Tahoe and have family in Brooklyn, New York, and Chino Hills, California. I would be open to accepting assignments in these areas as my traveling plans enable me.

I'm looking forward to establishing a business relationship with you in the near future. My contact information is listed above for your convenience.

✳ ✳ ✳ ✳

Bob Dunn
1313 Mockingbird Dr.
Phoenix, AZ 85047
Phone & Fax: (480) 470-9865
Pager/Mobile: (480) 550-1235
e-mail: Bdunn@msn.com

LETTER OF INTENT—MYSTERY SHOPPER

Let me introduce myself:

I received my B.A. degree in Business Administration from the University of Colorado and began a career in corporate, agency, and media advertising/marketing. I have had business relationships with leading companies and with all levels of their employees throughout the country. In addition to my exceptional verbal and written communications skills, I have the ability to recognize problems and substandard performance. I am a detail-minded perfectionist. I retired in 1998 and am now a licensed Realtor in Arizona. I work only part-time, and I am open to a variety of assignments, with preferences being hotels/resorts, restaurants, sporting events, financial, airline, and real estate.

Best and Worst Shopping Experiences

Best—I recently joined a health club. The young lady interviewed me regarding my health, medications, restrictions, and objectives. She then set up a program for flexibility, strength, and cardiovascular. She showed me how to train and gave me a diary to record each session. She was thorough and attentive . . . and demonstrated a sincere concern for my well-being. . . . I would strongly recommend this club to others due to the exceptional service she provided.

Worst—trying to get an airline ticket from an incompetent representative at the airline's ticket office. She didn't listen to what I wanted to do using my frequent flyer miles, and she made a mistake on the ticket she issued. I had to make another trip (30 miles) to get corrections and a new ticket. When my American Express statement arrived, there were incorrect charges because of her errors. [Tell the story here and state the facts only . . . discuss lack of organization rather than stating your opinion of her incompetence.]

Places I Am Willing to Visit

Any location in Ahwatukee, Arizona, which is a suburb of Phoenix. I am available to shop in Chandler, Tempe, Mesa, and Gilbert. I am also willing to travel the Phoenix metro area, and throughout the state depending on the assignment fee. In addition, I frequently visit my children in Los Angeles and South Dakota. I am also free to travel nationally for special assignments.

Thank you for considering my qualifications.

Bob Dunn

＊ ＊ ＊ ＊

To Whom It May Concern:

My name is Tom Brown. I would like to represent your company as a mystery shopper.

I am a high school science teacher. I have a Bachelor of Science in Applied Science and a Master's Degree in Science, and I hold my certificate in Principalship and Supervision in science education.

My teaching experience has been 16 years. I have taught science in a variety of settings, as well as regular education third grade. In addition, on a part-time basis, I have worked for a major chain grocery store in a variety of departments, worked for another major chain retail store, and held various temporary clerical positions, and I am a basketball instructor and coach basketball.

I am a very organized, detail-oriented people person. I have a great deal of experience writing numerous detailed reports that follow district, state, and federal guidelines and in analyzing various skills of students as required in my current position. Thoroughness and dependability are important to me in any endeavor that I am involved in.

Quality customer service is the key to creating and maintaining a quality business. From having worked in the retail business and as a customer, I realize the importance of having conscientious employees and how they reflect on the business. I enjoy making people happy and seeing friendly people doing their job satisfactorily. I would be an integral part of improving communication within the business.

My best shopping experience involved a business in which each employee that I came into contact with was extremely helpful, friendly, and courteous. They were focused on making suggestions that reasonably corresponded to my needs without expressing frustration or rushing my decisions and were thoughtful in answering my questions.

My worst shopping experience took place in an expensive, well-known restaurant in town that I had visited several times. It was an early weekend dinner. The waiter seemed quite annoyed at having to serve our table. He was extremely inattentive, had very little to say while serving, did not inquire if the food was to our satisfaction, and did not visit the table frequently to refill water glasses or refresh coffee. When requests were made, he would not follow through in a timely manner. The bill was delivered without a thank you or greeting of any type. It was quite disappointing.

I currently live in the southeastern region of Phoenix, Arizona, and I am familiar with the west and southwest part of the valley as well. I am willing to travel to various areas as needed for a shopping experience. I also travel to Seattle, Washington, and Tulsa, Oklahoma, occasionally and would be willing to shop those areas as well.

I am looking forward to establishing a business relationship with you in the near future and look forward to hearing from you.

Sincerely,
Tom Brown
2107 Baseline Rd.
Phoenix, AZ 85044
(480) 940-7706
TBrown@hotmail.com

* * * *

Letter of Intent

Are you looking for a mystery shopper who is dedicated, has strong customer service skills, is detail-oriented, and follows directions? I am a college graduate with a B.A. in Finance and Accounting, with recent Administrative Justice studies at Phoenix College. I am an Army veteran who served in the Military Police and currently works in law enforcement in the Phoenix area. I am interested in mystery shopping because it is a challenge.

My best recent shopping experience was purchasing a washer and dryer. The salesperson acknowledged me, gave me his business card, and showed me the different models after I indicated what I was look-ing for. He allowed me to browse freely, but was readily available to answer questions when I had them. This gentleman was knowledge-able and wanted to help me purchase a washer and dryer. He sug-gested additional items, such as the extended warranty. This was a very positive and pleasant experience.

My worst recent shopping experience was at a grocery store. I was in the dairy section wanting to buy some eggnog, but there was none on the shelf. I talked to the dairy clerk. I inquired whether the store had any more in stock. The employee was curt, indifferent, and sharp, and did not really want to help me find any eggnog. When I wanted to know if an additional delivery of eggnog would be arriving before the holidays, the clerk continued to be indifferent and made no attempt to contact any other store employee who would know. It was a very unpleasant experience.

If I were a mystery shopper for your clients, they would benefit by enhancing and improving their customer service image, leading to increased sales and improved profits. I am primarily interested in working in the Phoenix metropolitan area, but I can travel occasion-ally to other areas if needed. I have no limitations on my availability to perform shops for you or your clients.

Yours truly,
Frank Rose
2745 W. Lincoln Dr.
Phoenix, AZ 85046
(H) (480) 940-7251

※　※　※　※

Letter of Intent

Good day; my name is Diane Carpenter, and I am interested in becoming a mystery shopper for your organization. I have a wealth of experience in several areas, such as business, marketing, operations, management, and system development. I believe customer service is a key performance indicator for any company selling to or servicing consumers. I also believe the most reliable information that any com-pany can obtain comes from a customer, for it is the truth, customers don't lie. What a company does with this information can make or break its future.

My best shopping experience was at the Four Seasons in Seattle. What a wonderful place to stay. The entire staff was exceptionally polite, it was ready to grant my every wish, and did so. It was a pleasure to be treated as so special. Not once did they let me down, and they actually exceeded my expectations. A cab was ready for me on time, my shoes were shined every morning, and I looked forward to my nightly bed turndown, when I would walk into my room to hear the soft music as the day wound down.

My worst shopping experience was with North Eastern Airlines in Detroit. I requested an upgrade, was denied, and was literally followed onto the plane by a ticket agent to ensure that I would not sit in an open first-class seat. This was embarrassing to say the least, as I was a frequent flier. I was following the same process that I used in other cities; why was Detroit so different? I don't know to this day, but the flight attendant on the plane apologized and upgraded me as requested.

I am located in Phoenix, Arizona, and I am interested in mystery shopping for you in Ahwatukee, Phoenix, Tempe, Chandler, and Mesa. I frequently travel to Casa Grande and Tucson, Arizona, and I periodically travel to Michigan, Ohio, Washington, and California.

I am truly looking forward to working with you and assisting you with your company's customer service goals.

Sincerely,
Diane Carpenter
4261 E. Broadway Rd.
Phoenix, AZ 85052
Phone: (480) 894-3498
Email Diane007@aol.com

CHAPTER 4

Methods of Making Contact

There are several methods by which you can contact a company. First, the Internet is a tool that is being utilized more frequently in the form of message boards for acquiring leads, online applications for companies, and email. Next, there is the telephone for calling 800 numbers and stating your intent orally. In addition, a fax machine can fax your composed letter of intent. Finally, there is the U.S. Postal Service; you can mail out your letter of intent. Do not fear, you do not need to be computer literate to be a mystery shopper. Included in this chapter is a list of over 100 companies that do not use the Internet. Whatever your choice of contact method, I guarantee that you will find this chapter extremely helpful on your journey to becoming a mystery shopper. A strong word for success is apply, apply, and apply! I frequently hear the comment, "I applied to several companies, and I haven't heard anything back." Well, my first response would be: How many is several? If you invest 15 minutes in a new career, what do you expect to get out of it? Therefore, I recommend applying to or making at least 10 contacts a day for 30 days. Instead of watching an hour of TV each evening, invest the time in launching your new career and bettering yourself. If you take this advice, your phone will be ringing off the hook the following month.

The Internet

The Internet is an easy and cost-effective way to begin making contacts. There are several different methods of making contacts on the Internet, including message boards, online applications, and emails.

Message Boards

Message boards are also known as boards, electronic bulletin boards, forums, threads, and discussion boards. Message boards are an Internet-based form of communication that allows participants to post messages to a web site. When participants post messages on a message board, others may read and respond to them by posting their own messages.

   Message boards can be used for acquiring new assignments, discovering issues in the industry, and offering or receiving assistance. First, schedulers use these boards to post assignments that need to be completed immediately. For whatever reason, a shopper has withdrawn acceptance of an assignment, and the scheduler is in a bind. These assignments are taken rapidly, but you can use the information to establish contact with a company as a future shopper. Next, the industry is forever changing, and it is up to you to be aware of certain issues that are arising. For example, a couple of years ago, there was a bill on the floor of Congress (HB2444) that would have made it illegal to complete

```
Subj: Leads #60
Date: 9-3-03
From: ShopNet

----Sponsor--------------------
2 messages this issue

1. Apt. Shop
   OakCreek, WI
   from: Aptnet.org

2. Restaurants-TX, MD, AL
   EatShop.net
--------------------------------
Message 1
   Date 9-2-03
Have 2 Apts. available 9/10-9/15
$15 fee pd. in 30 days
```

integrity assignments without a private investigator's license. The bill did not pass, but it was close. Finally, if you are in need of help, you may ask questions on a message board, or you may answer a need for assistance. One example is asking about experience with a specific company in terms of, "Has anyone had experience with ABC mystery shopping company?" This information can be helpful if you have some concerns.

There are three methods of utilizing a message board. The first method is physical viewing of the site. One simply enters the Web address and views the message board. The next method is receiving individual emails. Every time a message is placed on the board, you will receive an email. The final method is the digest, in which when 25 messages accumulate on the board, you will receive one bulk email that summarizes senders and subject sections in chronological order, with the detailed listing at the end of the message, as depicted on the previous page. If there is nothing to your liking in the summary, then you can delete the entire message without having to read through the details.

Here are two brief examples:

From: scheduler1@abcscheduling.com

RE: Shopper needed in Orange County, California
    Shopper needed to visit retail store in Tustin, California. You must make a purchase of $5.00 and visit three departments in the store. Shop must be completed before October 16, and store must be visited between 5 and 8 p.m. The shop fee is $20 with a reimbursement of $5.00 for your purchase.
    If interested, please contact Susie at scheduler1@abcscheduling.com

※ ※ ※ ※

From: customerfriendly@customerfriendly.com

RE: Shopper needed in Phoenix, Arizona
    Shopper needed in Phoenix, Arizona, to visit an apartment complex in South Phoenix. The shopper must be Hispanic and speak fluent Spanish. The fee is $30.00, and the assignment requires a telephone call as well as a visit to the property. The report is a short one-page narrative with a three-page questionnaire.
    Please contact Sally at customerfriendly@friendly.com.

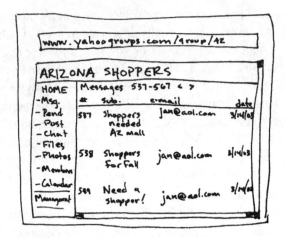

Lists of Message Boards

You can earn how to use message boards by taking a tour of:

Delphi: forums.delphiforums.com/dir-html/tour/page1_introduction.htm

MSN: groups.msn.com

Using Message Boards for Finding Leads

Check these boards on a daily basis for opportunities to shop in your area. Job postings are made daily and usually receive many replies, so keep trying. You can get started in mystery shopping much faster this way than by waiting for companies to contact you. Bookmark these pages and review them daily for new assignments. Good luck!

Leads-Only Message Boards

Yahoo! by NCPMS

http://clubs.yahoo.com/clubs/mysteryshoppingbyncpms

MS Leads by Elizabeths

http://www.delphi.com/msleadslist/messages

Mystery-Shopping Message Boards

Just Shop by NCPMS

http://www.delphi.com/justshop/start

Yahoo! by NCPMS
http://clubs.yahoo.com/clubs/mysteryshoppingbyncpms

MS Shops by Towanda
http://www.delphi.com/msshopnews/start

MS United by Elizabeth L.
http://forums.delphi.com/mshoppersunite/start

Lori's Undercover Shoppers
www.groups.msn.com/UndercoverShoppers

Mystery Shopping News on Delphi
forums.delphiforums.com/msshopnews/start

Mystery Shopping Talk on Delphi
forums.delphiforums.com/mysterytalk/start

Mystery Shopping United on Delphi
forums.delphiforums.com/mshoppersunite/start

MSPA Mystery Shoppers
www.mysteryshop.org/shoppers.php

Volition Mystery Shoppers
www.volition.com/mystery.html

Canadian Mystery Shoppers on Delphi
forums.delphiforums.com/canshoppers/start

Canada Mystery Shoppers on Delphi
forums.delphiforums.com/caroleburns2/start

Cathy's Corner Merchandising on Delphi
forums.delphiforums.com/cathyscorner2/start

Mystery Shop by Janeen
http://clubs.yahoo.com/clubs/mysteryshopping

Links 4U2C by Lisa
http://www.delphi.com/links4u2c/start

Julies—Highly Recommended
http://www.msr.builderspot.com/page/page/701306.htm

Merchandising Boards

Justshop by NCPMS
http://www.delphi.com/justshop/start

Merchandisers by Elizabeth L.
http://www.delphi.com/merchandising

Yahoo! by NCPMS
http://clubs.yahoo.com/clubs/mysteryshoppingbyncpms

Shop Board by Kendal
http://forums.delphi.com/mshopboard/messages

Merchandising by Pimms
http://www.delphi.com/Pimms/start

Mystery Shopping and Merchandising Boards

MS by Marsha
http://groups.yahoo.com/group/mysteryshopsupdate

Mystery Shopper by Cyndi
http://www.topica.com/lists/mysteryshopper

MS United by Elizabeth L.
http://www.topica.com/lists/mysteryshoppersunited

MS Openings by Stacey
http://www.topica.com/lists/MSopenings

MOM! by Julie Rogers
http://www.topica.com/lists/mom

Merchandisers by Elizabeth L.
http://www.topica.com/lists/MerchandisersListHere/

Shoppers by Alisa L.

http://groups.yahoo.com/group/Sshoppers

Lots-o-Fun by Amy

http://www.lots-o-fun.com/ms.htm

Mystery Shopping and Merchandisers on Yahoo

groups.yahoo.com/group/mysteryshoppingbyncpms

Shopping and Merchandising Newsletter on Topica

www.topica.com/lists/ncpms

Amy's Mystery Shoppers on Yahoo

groups.yahoo.com/group/lots-o-funms

Mystery Shoppers and Merchandisers on Topica

www.topica.com/lists/mysteryshopper

Mystery Shopping Openings on Topica

www.topica.com/lists/MSopenings

Mom's Mystery Shoppers on Topica

www.topica.com/lists/mom

Mystery Shoppers United on Topica

www.topica.com/lists/mysteryshoppersunited

Board Etiquette

Try to remember that you are applying for a job that requires great writing skills. If a company requests a writing sample, you should strive to present your *best* effort.

- DO NOT WRITE IT IN ALL CAPS (it looks like you are shouting).
- Do not write in all lowercase (it looks sloppy and unprofessional).
- If asked for a written paragraph, do not write in bullet style.
- One sentence is not a paragraph.

- Always use spell check.

- You should strive to appear organized. The company should not have to search for your contact information in the midst of a long, run-on paragraph with no punctuation.

- Please provide *all* of the requested information in the manner that the company requires.

- Send your request to the specified email address. Do not assume that you are replying to the sender. If you simply hit reply, you will be posting your information to the entire message board.

- The location(s) you are requesting should be apparent (either in the subject line or somewhere in the body of your email request).

- Respond only to those postings that you will be able to complete immediately. Remember, these boards are typically used for assignments that need to be completed yesterday. Do not respond to an assignment in Colorado because you will be there next month.

- Do not post negative statements about a mystery shopping agency, especially if your issue with that agency is unresolved. However, you may ask for help with an issue.

- Do not post "me too's!" It is annoying and creates excessive postings.

- Do not ask who shops whom; it violates confidentiality agreements. However, you may state that you have a car problem and need assistance finding a mystery shop that may cover some of your expenses.

- Try to remain positive and offer assistance.

- Types of viewing: direct email, digest, and physical viewing of web pages.

- Do not get caught up in negative discussions. Many people use boards to start verbally abusive wars; do not get involved.

Email Lists for Finding Leads

Email lists are known as e-lists, lists, Web-lists, and subscription lists. An email list is a list of email addresses of participants who want to send and receive email messages about a specific topic. When a message is sent to the email list, it is automatically distributed to all the subscribers. A participant must subscribe to an email list in order to begin sending and receiving messages.

This section gives instructions for subscribing and unsubscribing to email lists. Many postings are made to these lists on a daily basis. Usually the state is posted in the subject of the email. When you see your state or city listed, follow the instructions in the email for contacting the company. Be careful to respond to the company and not to the email list. Make it a habit not to just hit reply and send, or your email may get sent to hundreds of other shoppers instead of the intended company.

To subscribe to a list, simply send an email to the list name with -subscribe inserted before the @ symbol. You do not need to write anything in the body or the regarding section. You will then receive a reply email asking if you really wanted to subscribe to this list. Simply hit reply and send, and you will start to receive leads.

To subscribe to a list, use this format:

listname-subscribe@group.com

Example for first list:

mystery-shopper-subscribe@onelist.com

To unsubscribe, use this format:

listname-unsubscribe@group.com

To set list to digest so that you receive one email each day instead of several:

listname-digest@group.com

With Delphi, AOL, One-list, Topica, and Yahoo!, you must become a member of the domain in order to view any message boards or e-groups. I am the monitor of Arizonashoppers@yahoogroups.com. In order to join this group, you must first become a member of Yahoo!, which of course is free. You can register at www.yahoo.com.

The following question was posed by one of my students:

Undercover Shoppers Article—August 2003

Help please Dr. Newhouse,

I have been trying to subscribe to something called a message board, and I have been having problems. Do I have to join a club or something before I can subscribe to the free boards?

Thanks!

Traci

Ahwatukee, AZ

* * * *

Good Day Traci,

The message boards are a wonderful way to enter the field of mystery shopping. Additionally, using the message boards is the fastest method for starting a mystery shopping career.

A message board or leads list is similar to a bulletin board at a community center or unemployment office. Some boards are totally restricted, and only a select few people can put postings on the board or look at the board. Others are totally open, so that anyone can view or put messages on the board. However, just as with a bulletin board, you have to physically enter the building and approach the board to look at the board.

Therefore, if the board is sponsored by a server such as AOL, Delphi, Yahoo!, or Excite, then you must join the server before you can view or join the boards. There is no cost for joining the servers or the boards. For example, my group, arizonashoppers@yahoogroups.com, is an open group. You must first register with www.yahoo.com, and then you are free to join the group by sending a blank email to arizonashoppers-subscribe@yahoogroups.com. After you send an email, you will receive a message confirming your attempt to join. You simply hit reply and you will start receiving emails immediately.

These boards are utilized by schedulers and mystery shopping companies to post leads. The emails you will receive from the boards will mainly consist of leads or "want ads." Each time a message is placed on the board, you will receive a message in email form. Remember, this is a board that thousands of people view, so it is important not to immediately hit reply! If you simply hit reply, you will be responding to the entire board. Next, the emails are not personal messages to you. Therefore, if you do not wish to complete an assignment, there is no need to respond to the message. Additionally, you may receive emails requesting or providing helpful information about the industry. Finally, you may post messages to the board if you personally need assistance.

Remember, these boards are a quick way to get started; however, they should not be your primary source for finding leads or jobs.

Schedulers utilize these boards to fill assignments when a shopper has not followed through on a commitment, and thus the assignment needs to be completed yesterday. This results in a first-come, first-served basis, and if you are not an early riser and do not stare at the computer all day long, you will receive a lot of response messages stating that assignment has been filled. My recommendation is to personally contact or apply to as many companies as possible. You will then be listed in the databases of these companies and will be contacted before the jobs appear on the message boards.

Take care, and may peace be with you,

Dr. Ilisha Newhouse
Author, *Mystery Shopping Made Simple*
www.newhouseservices.com
ilisha@qwest.net

General Leads Lists

Search at topica.com and egroups.com for "mystery shopping"

mystery-shopper@onelist.com

secret-shopper@egroups.com

mysteryshopper@egroups.com

QualityShoppers@onelist.com

mysteryshopper@topica.com

MSOpenings@topica.com

ShopperMatch@egroups.com

JWRIGHT@egroups.com

MysteryShopping@egroups.com

shops-r-us@onelist.com

secretshoppers@egroups.com

Specific Region Mystery-Shopping Lists

Northeast Shoppers
Subscribe: NEShoppers-subscribe@yahoogroups.com

Mid-Atlantic Shoppers

Subscribe: MAShoppers-subscribe@yahoogroups.com

Central States Shoppers

Subscribe: CSShoppers-subscribe@yahoogroups.com

Great Lake States Shoppers

Subscribe: GLSShoppers-subscribe@yahoogroups.com

Pacific States Shoppers

Subscribe: PSShoppers-subscribe@yahoogroups.com

SoutheasternShoppers

Subscribe: SEShoppers-subscribe@yahoogroups.com

USA

USAmysteryshoppers-subscribe@yahoogroups.com

Lists by State

To receive email leads for your state only, send an email specifically tailored to your state. For example, I am the monitor of the Arizona list, Arizonashoppers@yahoogroups.com.

To receive the list for a state other than Arizona, simply substitute the name of that particular state; for example, NewYorkshoppers@yahoogroups.com.

To subscribe to a state list, you need to insert -subscribe after the state name and before the @ symbol. Send a blank email to this address and you will start receiving emails right away with assignments in your area.

Examples: Mail to: Arizonashoppers-subscribe@yahoogroups.com.

Additional Lists

111-Everythinguwant@onelist.com

390-jobs-offered@topica.com

Ads@homejobstop.com

Americashoppers@yahoogroups.com

AMY@homeworkers.org

ArizonaNetworking@yahoogroups.com

BeenzNFreebies@yahoogroups.com

californiashoppers@yahoogroups.com

CaMoms-owner@yahoogroups.com

CAN-MysteryShops@yahoogroups.com

CanShop@yahoogroups.com

cjsm0001@yahoo.com

cwhite@onelist.com

cwhite@yahoogroups.com

DC-MysteryShops@yahoogroups.com

FayeLin@aol.com

Frugal-Folks-Freebies@yahoogroups.com

illinoisNetworking@yahoogroups.com

illinoisshoppers@yahoogroups.com

ILMoms-owner@yahoogroups.com

info@double-check.com

IWANTWORK@topica.com

jmartynec@earthlink.net

JMoreau1@aol.com

jobs@mysteryshopperservices.com

JWright@onelist.com

jwright@topica.com

jwright88@msn.com

LilasLounge@yahoogroups.com

lots-o-funms@yahoogroups.com

LotsOShops@aol.com

MAshoppers@yahoogroups.com

MEP@topica.com

MichiganNetworking@yahoogroups.com

michiganshoppers@yahoogroups.com

MIMoms-owner@yahoogroups.com

MissouriNetworking@yahoogroups.com

missourishoppers@yahoogroups.com

MOM@topica.com

MOMoms-owner@yahoogroups.com

MS@topica.com

MS_Arizona@yahoogroups.com

MS_California@yahoogroups.com

ms_illinois@yahoogroups.com

ms_Michigan@yahoogroups.com

ms_Missouri@yahoogroups.com

ms_newyork@yahoogroups.com

msopenings@topica.com

mystery_shoppers@yahoogroups.com

MysteryMerch@listbot.com

MYSTERYSHOP@topica.com

mysteryshopper@egroups.com

mysteryshopper@onelist.com

MYSTERYSHOPPER@topica.com

mysteryshopper@yahoogroups.com

MysteryshopperII@topica.com

MYSTERYSHOPPERLL@topica.com

mysteryshoppersunited@topica.com

mysteryshopping@onelist.com

MysteryShopping@yahoogroups.com

Mysteryshoppingleads@onelist.com

Mysteryshoppingleads@yahoogroups.com

mysteryshops@eGroups.com

MYSTERYSHOPS@topica.com

mysteryshops@yahoogroups.com

Mystery-Shops@yahoogroups.com

mysteryshopsupdate@onelist.com

newyorkNetworking@yahoogroups.com

newyorkshoppers@yahoogroups.com

NYMoms-owner@yahoogroups.com

Posting@SuperShoppersGroup.com

QUALITYSHMEP@topica.com

qualityshoppers@egroups.com

qualityshoppers@onelist.com

QUALITYSHOPPERS@topica.com

qualityshoppers@yahoogroups.com

Secret-shopper@onelist.com

secret-shopper@yahoogroups.com

secretshoppers@onelist.com

secretshoppers@yahoogroups.com

secretshopping@topica.com

ShopArizona@topica.com

Shopillinois@topica.com

ShopMichigan@topica.com

ShopMissouri@topica.com

Shopnewyork@topica.com

Shoppermatch@onelist.com

shoppermatch@yahoogroups.com

shopperrecruiting@yahoogroups.com

SHOPPERS@TOPICA.COM

shoppersresources@egroups.com

ShoppingArizona@topica.com

SHOPPINGCALIFORNIA@topica.com

Shoppingillinois@topica.com

ShoppingMichigan@topica.com

ShoppingMissouri@topica.com

Shoppingnewyork@topica.com

shoprequest@mysteryshops.com

shops-r-us@onelist.com

shops-r-us@yahoogroups.com

socalshops@yahoogroups.com

sonyasmysteryshoppers@home.com

sshopper@yahoogroups.com

sshoppers@onelist.com

sshoppers@yahoogroups.com

SUPERSHOPPERS@mailcity.com

telecommute-telework@onelist.com

telecommute-telework@yahoogroups.com

THEPOSTS@avon.net

Theschedulers@onelist.com

USAmysteryshoppers@yahoogroups.com

USAshoppers@topica.com

VAMSleads@onelist.com

weneedshoppers@topica.com

yiwhjoblist@topica.com

Distribution Lists

There are several organizations that compose lists of shoppers and then match shoppers to organizations in need. These lists usually charge a fee and are the number-one source of scams. The only reputable list I have found in this industry is called Select a Shopper. The fee is approximately $25, and it is distributed to over 200 organizational members. I joined this list many years ago and paid $25, and to this date I am still receiving assignments from this source.

You can contact Select a Shopper at :

www.SelectaShopper.com

3237A E. Sunshine #167

Springfield, MO 65804

Phone (417) 848-7831

Email: Matt@selectashopper.com

Other Referral services

Julie's Bathrobebiz for Shoppers: www.bathrobebiz.com

Shadow Shopper Referral Service: shadowshopper.com/?rid=%CD%A4%7Fr

Select a Shopper Referral Service: www.selectashopper.com

Lead Manager for Shoppers: www.leadmgr.com

Scheduling Services

Palm Scheduling Services: www.palmschedulingservices.com

Coast to Coast Scheduling Services: www.ctcss.com

Dawn Hunt: www.deltadeveloping.net/dawnhunt/

Newsletters

Undercover Shoppers: undercovershopper@hotmail.com or http://groups.msn.com/UndercoverShoppers

Support Services and Groups

NCPMS Support Services

Learning Center Forum for Shoppers & Merchandisers: www. ncpmscenter.org/forum

Justshop for Shoppers & Merchandisers: forums.delphiforums. com/justshop/start

Other Great Support Services and Groups

Melanie Mystery Shopping Coach: www.mysteryshoppercoach.com

Julie's Bathrobebiz for Shoppers: www.bathrobebiz.com

Lori's Undercover Shoppers: groups.msn.com/UndercoverShoppers

Volition Mystery Shoppers: www.volition.com/mystery.html

Alyice E. Mystery Shoppers: thedabblingmum.com/work_mystery_shopper.htm

Sonya's Mystery Shoppers: www.sonyasmysteryshoppers.com

Susan Perry's Mystery Shoppers: www.professionalmysteryshoppers.com

Learning Opportunities for Mystery Shopping and Merchandising Professionals

NCPMS Learning Center: www.ncpmscenter.org

MSPA: www.mysteryshop.org

BrainBench E-Learning: www.brainbench.com

LearnFree.com: www.learnfree.com

Barnes & Nobles University: www.bnuniversity.com

A Commonly Asked Question

What is the difference between the NCPMS and the MSPA?
Thanks,

Ethel
Gilbert, Arizona

✳ ✳ ✳ ✳

Good day Ethel,

Thank you for the wonderful question. The NCPMS stands for the National Center for Professional Mystery Shoppers. It is an organization of shoppers for shoppers. In other words, it is made for us by us. The president is Niccole Rogers, and she is an intelligent and kind woman. The main web site is www.justshop.com, and it has a wealth of information. The organization offers tutorials, leads, assistance, training, and mediation. For example, if you have an issue about getting paid, it would represent you for free. Additionally, the NCPMS offers online certification programs, and I am on the board of education, which establishes criteria for certification. I also teach a certification course at South Mountain Community College in my home state of Arizona. Anyone can join this organization, including shoppers, schedulers, and mystery shopping companies. The organization is open-minded and will help anyone on his or her individual journey. It offers annual awards to the best of the best such as the Best Mystery Shopping Company or Shopper of the Year. What ever your needs may be, this organization will go out of its way to help you.

The MSPA is the Mystery Shopper Providers Association and is an organization of mystery shopping companies for mystery shopping companies. It mainly offers assistance to companies; however, there is a wonderful feature on the web site that allows a shopper to search for companies by industry, country, or state. For example, if I wanted to shop hotels in California, I could run a search for hotels in the state of California and it would provide a list of every mystery shopping company that has hotel accounts in the state of California. Additionally, if you receive an assignment for a five-star hotel for one week, you might want to contact this organization and ask if there have been any complaints about the company in question. The MSPA offers a training program as well, which I believe is entitled "Gold Certification." I have heard a rumor that the MSPA plans to have all its members hire only shoppers who have taken this program; however, this is not yet the case, for it has offered this program only a few times. Although this may be the MSPA's future intention, please keep in mind that this organization has only a little over 100 members and that there are over 750 mystery-shopping companies in the continental United States alone, not to mention several in Canada. The web site for the MSPA is www.mysteryshop.org.

The two organizations sponsor different programs and have different agendas pertaining to their specific populations. Therefore, they are colleagues rather than competitive in nature. Additionally, they both have annual conventions with training and recognition. These two organizations offer a wealth of information as well as free assistance. A shopper can gain benefits from both organizations.

Take care of yourself, and may peace and love be with you always.

Online Applications

Many companies are converting to full use of the Internet, meaning that you can apply to the organization, accept assignments, and enter reports online. Basically, you enter the company web site and click on the section for future shoppers. It is important to scan the information requested before filling out the application because the company may ask for information you that may not want to provide. A good example is your social security number. If you are uncomfortable providing your social security number over the Internet, then you will need to fill out an SS-4 and acquire an employer identification number as an alternative to using your social security number. It is perfectly legal for the company to ask for social security information because it needs the information for tax purposes. If you make over $600 per year from one company, it must file a form 1099. We will discuss this issue in Chapter 8. Nonetheless, if you are uncomfortable giving all the information, then do not apply. If you leave questions blank, the company will not contact you because this industry is solely based on assessments and your ability to fill out a form. So do not waste your time filling out partial applications.

Additionally, you may be asked your sex, age, annual income, number of children, number of pets, marital status, and other such questions. This information is needed to match you to specific assignments. For example, if you are 65, you might look odd in a college bar or a Hooters restaurant, or if you are in your twenties you might look odd purchasing orthopedic shoes or visiting a retirement home. During the process, you will be asked all the questions we discussed when we covered the letter of intent. This is why it is important to compose the letter of intent so that you are not writing the same information numerous times. You can simply copy the information from the letter of intent and paste it into the online application.

Another commonly asked question is this:

Hi Dr. Newhouse, hope your Monday is going well. It is Sue with a question for you!

I logged on to one of the discussion groups at Delphi. I was just reading past posts when one caught my eye, and I am now confused. The post was about the discussion group revealing which company mystery shops for a particular grocery store. One of the participants was angry that the members had revealed the answer to each other. This person said it was a breach of the confidentiality agreement signed by shoppers for that company.

My question is this: On several of my recent applications to companies, I have been asked who else have I shopped for and how many times. It didn't occur to me that this could be a breach in confidentiality. What do you think? If I leave the space blank, they might throw out the entire application. Thanks for your input, as always, you keep me going! I have two more little shops to do now; they are a snap compared to the paperwork involved in that hotel shop I told you about. Well, live and learn, right?

Thanks so very much,

Sue

* * * *

Hi Sue!

That is a fantastic question. First, I typically answer that question by stating that I have been a shopper for over 5 years and have worked for over 200 different market research agencies. Specific names shall be submitted upon request.

You can state which mystery-shopping companies you have worked for in the past. You can even go so far as to that state you did fastfood assignments for ABC Mystery Shopping Company. However, you cannot state that you did Burger King assignments for ABC Mystery Shopping Company. You can never state that you did a specific facility for a specific mystery shopping company, for this is in violation of your confidentiality agreement and you could be subject to a variety of legal and monetary consequences.

Company Listings

MaFixIt by Karen:

http://members.aol.com/mafixit/mysteryshop/ index.html.

Mafixit is by far the most recommended web site for company listings. When you first view the web site, you will notice various advertisements. Pan down a page or two, and you will see a section that lists the letters of the alphabet. If you click on the letter A, you will receive a listing of all mystery-shopping companies beginning with the letter A that have Internet access and web sites for applying online. I recommend that you start with the letters S, C, M, and N.

Additional Company Listings

MOM! by Julie Rogers: www.mom-mom.com/making.htm

Merchandiser by JoAnn: http://www.freeyellow.com/members6/jonys/page1.html

Shopping 4 Free by Janeen: http://www.shopping4free.net/companies.htm

NARMS: http://www.narms.com

Lots-o-Fun by Amy: http://www.lots-o-fun.com/ms.htm

Mystery Shopping Companies by Arlana: www.100megsfree3. com/arlana/mystery.htm

Market Research Association—Blue Book Directory—Sort by MS Services: http://www.bluebook.org/CompanyResults.CFM? RequestTimeout=500

Zarden—Sort by Mystery Shopping Services: http://www.zarden. com/marketresearch/services/myster-a.html

Mystery Shop Island: http://www.mysteryshopisland.com /compa-nya-e.html

Once you have applied online, the company will contact you with a welcome aboard message. In most cases you will be provided with a password and notified when assignments are posted to the web site. You will then visit the web site and enter your password. When you have reviewed the assignments and selected the desired ones, you will receive a confirmation and additional information, such as instruc-tions and forms. Finally, you will complete the assignment and enter the data online. It is a completely paperless process! Do not assume that all companies work this way just because they have a web site, and make sure that you verify the scheduling process and procedure.

Self-Scheduling Systems

The SASSIE and PROPHET systems are software systems that are the result of a joint effort by many companies to establish industry software. You can register and self-schedule assignments via the SASSIE or PROPHET system. After you register, you will receive a notice with your user name and password. The company will then email you a notice stating that assignments have been posted. You visit the web site and enter your user name and password. You select the assignments you want, and you will receive a confirmation that you have been selected as the evaluator. All information is posted on this web site, including instructions, sample forms, and the online entry form. You must view the instructions and sample forms, then visit the assigned location. After completing the visit, you can enter the data online, and you will receive a confirmation number. This process is completely paperless and is def-initely the future direction of the mystery shopping industry.

Here is a list of shopper frequently asked questions from the Sassieshop web site:

1. *Who is Sassie? Am I working for Sassieshop.com?* No, you are working for mystery-shop providers who have chosen SASSIE as their software system. SassieShop.com and SurfMerchants are the publishers of the SASSIE mystery-shopping system software. We do not schedule shops or process payments to mystery shoppers (we only provide support for system wide technical issues).

2. *Where are the SASSIE jobs posted?* Currently, SASSIE works on an email invitation system. Shop invitations matching your location (and possibly your gender) will be emailed directly to you. If you are interested in the shop, there is a web address provided where you can apply for the shop.

3. *Why should I save my survey every 30 minutes?* Regularly saving your work in SASSIE helps to ensure that you won't lose data if you lose your Internet or dial-up connection. Also, your SASSIE login will expire after 60 minutes without a submission. Therefore, to avoid losing your data, we recommend you save your surveys every 30 minutes. Even if your submission is incomplete, your survey answers have been saved and you can continue working on it until it's complete.

4. *Who do I call/email for assistance?* While we enjoy talking to shoppers, the volume of shoppers using the SASSIE system makes it impossible for us to respond to individual requests. Please contact the mystery-shop provider you are working for directly for assistance. Please do not call or email Sassieshop.com or SurfMerchants with individual shopper support issues, as we cannot respond directly.

Exception: If, while using SASSIE, you experience an error message that instructs you to email an error message to Sassieshop.com or Surfmerchants.com, please do email us—we do appreciate the assistance.

5. *I tried to apply for a shop, but I got a "Page not found" error. Link in email doesn't work?* Some email programs break up long internet addresses across two lines. In this case, clicking on the link

will not bring you to the correct location. *Solution*: Copy the *entire* link and paste it into your browser to make the link work.

6. *I got a Shopper Grade on my shop—what does it mean*? SASSIE gives reviewers the option to grade a survey from 1 to 10 (or to give no grade at all). Each mystery shop uses these grades differently, so a score of 6 may be a good score for one mystery shop and a bad score for another. If the mystery shop does use shopper grades, as a new shopper you will automatically be assigned a shopper grade of 5. In most cases, shopper grading is a tool to give more shops to the hardest-working shoppers.

Note: If a shop received no grade at all, it does *not* get factored into your Shopper Rating Average.

7. *Do I have to sign up/login for each mystery shopping provider separately? How can I find other companies that use SASSIE?* Unfortunately, you *do* have to sign up for each company separately, and we cannot reveal all of our subscribers (although we would love to). Our confidentiality agreements prevent us from doing either of these at this time.

8. *Which companies utilize the SASSIE system*?

Cirrus Marketing Group

Eyes R Us

IntelliShop

Jancyn—For apartment shopping database

Kern Scheduling Services

Merc Systems

Mystique Shoppers

Service Excellence Group

Service Performance Group

SG Marketing

Who Uses Self-Assigning?

Self-assigning means that you schedule shops for yourself without having to go through a scheduler. Most mystery shoppers *love* companies that allow them to do this, but it does make things much more competitive. Here's a list of self-assigning mystery-shopping sites. Please visit the "A" list for web sites.

Beyond Hello	Ken-Rich Retail Group
Business Evaluation Services	Maritz Research
Certified Reports, Inc.	Mercantile Systems and Surveys
Check Mark, Inc.	Pinkerton
A Closer Look	Pulseback
Confero	Sensors Quality Management
Corporate Research, Int.	Service Evaluation Concepts
Ellis Property Management Systems	Service Intelligence
Eye on Retail	SG Marketing
Feedback Plus	Shop'n Check
ICC/Decision Services	Shoppers Critique Int.
Imyst	Sights on Service
Infotel	Solomon Group
JM Ridgeway	Trend Source

Emailing Individual Companies

Sending an email to an individual company is an excellent method of indicating your intent to shopping agencies. You can simply compose a cover letter or note in an email and then attach your letter of intent to the email. You can send your letter to over 50 companies at one time if you separate each address with a semicolon (;) and a space. Additionally, I recommend that you send it blind carbon copy, or BCC, so that each individual company is unaware that you are sending the same email out to 50 other companies and so that it has a professional appearance.

The "A" List

The following is a list of over 400 companies with strong ethics that value the individual shopper as a key component of business success. All mystery-shopping companies were provided with the opportunity to be listed as a business that is ethical and several chose not to be listed. However, you may find the additional 350 companies by going to the links given under "Company Listings."

Here is a list of over 400 companies you can apply to online or via email:

Company Web Site or Email Address

Company	Web Site or Email Address
A & M Business Services	http://www.ambussvcs.com/
A Closer Look, Inc	http://www.a-closer-look.com/
A Customer's Point of View	http://www.mindspring.com/ ~mysteryshopping
A Total Resource Group (email link)	totalresourcegrp@aol.com
A&A Merchandising Ltd	http://www.aamerch.com/
A&S Field Services	hl12190@aol.com
A.I.M. Field Service	www.patsaim.com
AC Nielsen	http://www.acnielsen.ca/
Ace Mystery Shopping	http://www.acemystery shopping.com/
Acra, Inc	http://www.aq-services.com/
ActionLink	www.actionlink.biz
Advanced Retail Merchandising, Inc.	www.arm-retail.com
Advantage Sales & Marketing (email link)	boyd.stevens@asmcanada.com
Advisory Group, Inc (email link)	kassoff@advisorygroupinc.net
AIM Field Service	http://www.patsaim.com/
Alexandria's Marketing	www.alexandriasmarketing. com
All-About Demo's Inc.	bobbie@olp.net
Alliance Marketing Group, LLC	tcaddell@mapnetwork.net
American Marketing Services	http://www.american marketing.com/

Amusement Advantage	http://www.amusement advantage.com/
Ann Michaels and Associates	http://www.ishopforyou.com/
Anonymous Insights	http://www.a-insights.com/ index2.html
Anonymous Shoppers & Assessments	http://www.asa pittsburgh.com/index2.htm
Apartment Shoppe	http://www.apartmentmystery shopper.com/
A-Plus Retail Services, Inc.	Aplus@isd.net
ARC Research Corporation	http://www.arcresearch.com/
Archon Development	http://prophetb1.archondev.com/ archon/web.nsf/
Ardent Services, Inc	www.ardentservices.com
Ask Southern California	http://www.asksocal.com/
At Your Service Marketing	http://www.aysm.com/
Ath Power Consulting Corporation	http://athpower.com/
Audits and Surveys Worldwide	http://www.surveys.com/
Ban Consult	http://www.banconsult.com/
Barry Leeds & Associates	http://www.barryleedsassoc.com/
Barry Promotions Inc.	www.barrypromotions.com
Best Mark	http://www.bestmark.com/
Best Service Company	http://www.bestservice company.com/
Better Marketing Associates (BMA)	http://www.mystery-shopping.com/
Beyond Hello	https://www.beyondhello.com/ secure/index.htm
Beyond Marketing Group	http://beyondmarketinggroup.com/
Blackstone Research Group, The	http://www.bgglobal.com/
BLD Scheduling Services	http://bldschedulers.com/
BMK, Inc.	jmoroze@bmkinc.com

Business Evaluation Services (BES)	http://www.mysteryshopper services.com/
Business Insights Group	http://www.businessinsights.com/
Business Research Lab	http://www.busreslab.com/ survey.htm
Business Resources	http://bizpublications.com/
Business Solutions	http://www.bizshoptalk.com/
Buyer's Choice	http://www.byerschoiceinc.com/
California Marketing Specialists	http://www.sassieshop.com/ 2californiamarketing
Campaigners, Inc.	www.campaigners.com
Campbell Edgar	http://www.retailmystery shoppers.com/mystery.html
Campus Consulting	http://www.shopaudits.com/
Canadian Merchandsing & Assembly Services	www.CMandAS.com
Capstone Research	http://www.capstoneresearch.com/
Carlene Research	http://www.carleneresearch.com/
Certified Reports Inc.	http://www.certifiedreports.com/
Channel Partners	www.channelpartners.com
Check Mark, Inc.	http://www.checkmarkinc.com/
Checker's Product Servicing, Inc.	www.checkersinc.com
Check-Up Marketing	https://www.checkup marketing.com/main.html
Christian Science Monitor, The	www.csmonitor.com
Chuck Latham Associates, Inc.	www.clareps.com
Cirrus Marketing Consultants	http://www.cirrusmktg.com/
CKA Group, Inc.	http://www.ckagroup.com/ home.html
Classic Demos, Inc.	www.classicdemos.com
Client First Associates	http://www.cf-associates.com/
Coast to Coast Scheduling Services	http://ctcss.com/

Commercial Services System	http://www.commercialservice systems.com/
Confero Mystery Shopping	www.conferoinc.com
Consumer Connection	http://www.consumer connection.net/
Consumer Direct	http://www.customerdirect.com/
Consumer Impressions, Inc.	http://consumer impressions.com/jobopp.htm
Consumer Research Group (CRG)	http://www.crg2000.com/
Consumer ST	http://www.customer-1st.com/
Contemporary Research Center	http://www.crcdata.com/
Corporate Research Group, The	http://www.thecrg.com/
Corporate Research International (CoRI)	http://www.mysteryshops.com/
Count on Us	http://www.ucountonus.com/
Courtesy Counts	http://courtesycounts.com/
Coyle Hospitality Group	http://www.coylehospitality.com/
Creative Channel Services, Inc.	www.creativechannel.com
Creative Image Associates, Inc.	http://www.creativeimage.net/
Critique International	http://www.critique international.com/
Cross Financial Group	http://crossfinancial.com/
Crossmark Canada	www.crossmark.com
CRS/Lawrence Service	www.crslawrence.com
Customer Point of View	http://www.mindspring.com/ ~mysteryshopping/evals.html
Customer Service Perceptions	http://www.csperceptions.com/
CV Marketing Research Inc.	http://www.cv-market.com/
CyberShop by Roper ASW	http://cybershoppers.surveys.com/
Demos Express	susan@demosexpress.com
Division21	www.division21.com
DSG Associates	www.dsgstars.com

DSI	www.DSIforce.com
E & K Enterprises, Inc.	www.stealingyoublind.com
Eagle Merchandising Services, Inc.	garye@elgaaen-booth.com
Elite Demonstration Service, LLC	eliteut@aol.com
Elite Retail Services, Inc.	www.eliteretail.com
Ellis Property Management Services	http://www.epmsonline.com/
Euro RSCG Impact	www.eurorscgimpact.com
Evaluation Systems for Personnel (ESP)	www.espshop.com
Eyes R Us, Inc.	http://www.eyesrusinc.com/
Feedback Plus, Inc.	http://www.gofeedback.com/
Field Facts Worldwide	http://www.fieldfacts.com/
Field Force, Inc., The	www.thefieldforce.com
Field Marketing, Inc.	www.fieldmktg.com
Field Merchandising Services, Inc.	fmsi@ncim.com
Fieldflex Merchandising, Inc.	www.fieldflex.com
First Bank	http://www.efirstbank.com/
Florida Retail Service, Inc.	mimi@ppi-frs.com
Focus on Service	http://www.focusonservice.com/
Force One Merchandising, Inc.	mmarano@force1one.com
Franchise Compliance, Inc.	http://www.franchise compliance.com/
Franklin Resource Group, Inc.	www.FranklinResource.com
Frontline Services	fline@woh.rr.com
FSA Merchandising Inc. (Field Surveys & Audits)	fsa@wi.rr.com
Full Scope Mystery Shopping	http://www.fullscopemystery shopping.com/
FYI Video Shops	www.fyivideoshops.com

Game Film Consultants Mystery Shopping	www.gamefilmconsultants.com
Genesis Group	http://www.genesisgrp.com/
Gerson Company, The	www.gersoncompany.com
Get Creative Marketing	http://www.getcreative marketing.com/
Globalteam International Marketing Consultants, Inc.	www.globalteam-usa.com
Golden Resources Marketing Group	http://members.aol.com/ cgr315/index.html
Gral-Iteo	meta.arh@email.si
Grantham, Orilio & Associates (GOA)	http://www.goashoppers.com/
Graymark Security Group	http://www.graymark security.com/web/
Green & Associates Mystery Shopping	http://www.greenand associates.com/
Greet America, Inc.	http://www.greetamerica.com/
Hauser(Mail Agent)	http://www.hausernet.com/
Hilli Dunlap Enterprises	http://www.dunlapenterprises.com/
Hindsight	http://www.hindsight.com/
HMI Associates	http://www.hmiassociates.com/
HOED Holdings Pty. Ltd.	http://www.hoedholdings.com.au/
Hoffmann & Forcher Marketing Research	wolfgang.forcher@hf.co.at
Hotel Shopping Network, The	www.hotelmysteryshopper.com
Howard Services	http://www.howard services.com/homess.html
HR and Associates	http://hrandassociates.com/
HR Options	www.hroptions.com
Huffy Service First	www.servicefirst.com
I MYST	http://www.imyst.com/
ICC/Decision Services	www.iccds.com
IMAGINUSINC	http://www.imaginusinc.com/
Imperial Distributors, Inc.	www.imperialdist.com

InCite Research & Marketing Solutions	http://www.incitemar.com/
ImEDGEexperts	Imedgeexperts@cox.net
Infotel	http://www.infotelinc.com/
Innovative Retail Services	www.innovativeretailserv.com
Instant Reply	http://www.mystery shopservices.com/
In-Store Marketing	jnance1941@aol.com
Integrity Auditing Services, Inc.	integauditsvs@aol.com
IntelliShop	www.internationalservice check.com/sitehtml/index.html
International Surveys	http://international surveys.8k.com/contact.html
J.R. Demos & Merchandising	www.//home.fuse.net/jrdemos
Jack in the Box Restaurants	http://www.jacksguest.com/
Jade Promotions & Marketing	www.jadepromotions.net
Jancyn Evaluation Shops	http://www.jancyn.com/
JC & Associates	http://www.jcandassociates.com/
JM Ridgeway	http://www.jmridgeway.com/
Joshua Research Consultants	joshuarc@singnet.com.sg
K.A.M Data Services	kamsrv@aol.com
Ken-Rich Retail Group	http://www.ken-rich.com/
Kern Scheduling Services	http://www.kernscheduling.com/
Kit Moss Productions, Inc.	www.kitmoss.com
KTR Group	www.ktrcreative.com
Lantis Merchandising Services (LMS)	www.lantismerchandising.com
Lasting Impressions	http://exitnow.com/lasting/ mystery_shopper_application.htm
Leadership Factor Ltd.,The	http://www.leadershipfactor.com/
LeBlanc & Associates	http://www.mleblanc.com/
Levy Merchandising Services	www.levyservices.com
Liberty Research Services	http://www.libertyresearch services.com/

Locksley Group Ltd.	http://www.locksleygroupltd.com/
Management Consultant Group, LLC	http://www.management consultantgroup.com/
Maritz	http://www.maritz.com/
Maritz Research—Virtuoso	http://www.virtuoso.maritz research.com/
Market Image	www.marketimageflorida. com
Market Resources, L.L.C.	emcinc@bellsouth.net
Market Trends	http://www.market trends.com/index.shtm
Market Viewpoint	http://www.marketviewpoint.com/
Marketing Endeavors, LLC	http://www.marketingendeavors. biz/
Marketing Solutions Int'l	www.marketingservicesinc.net
Marketing Systems	http://www.msultd.com/
Mar's Surveys	http://www.marsresearch.com/
Mass Connections	http://massconnections.com/
MCG Retail	www.mcg-retail.com
Mclinda Brody and Company	http://www.melindabrody.com/
Merchandise Concepts	http://www.merchandise concepts.com/
Merchandise Support Services	www.totalaccessmarketing. com
Merchandise Support, Inc. (MSI)	www.msico.com
Merchandisers for Hire	www.merchandisersforhire.com
Merchandising Advantage Plus	www.mapnetwork.net
Merchandising Corporation of America	www.mcaretail.com
Merchandising Specialists	www.merchspec.com
Michelson & Associates	http://www.michelson.com/ home.html
Mikes Mystery Shopping Service	http://www.angelfire.com/ pa/mystershopper/

Mind Gym, Inc.	http://mindgyminc.com/
Mintel International Group, Ltd.	http://www.services.mintel.com/
Mosaic Info Force	http://www.mosaic-infoforce.com/
Mosaic Sales Solutions	www.mosaicsalessolutions.com
Mosaic Sales Solutions—Irvine	www.mosaic.com
Muscle Marketing	gigi@ix.netcom.com
Mystery Guest	http://www.mysteryguestinc.com/
Mystery Shopper Metropark	http://www.metropark.com/ nggroup/
Mystery Shoppers	http://www.mystery-shoppers.com/
Mystery Shoppers, Inc.	http://www.mysteryshoppersinc.com/
Mystery Shopping 411	www.mysteryshopping411.com
Mystery Shopping Solutions, Inc.	http://www.mystshopsol.com/
Mystery Surfer	www.mystery-surfing.com
Mystique Shopper	http://www.mystiqueshopper.com
National Marketing Services	www.natlmktg.com
National MegaForce	www.nationalmegaforce.com
National Retail Services	www.nrs3.com
National Shopping Service	http://www.nationalshopping service.com/
National Shopping Service Network	http://www.mysteryshopper.net/
Nationwide Integrity Services Inc.	http://www.nationwideintegrity.com
Nationwide Services Group, Inc. (NSG)	http://www.nationwidesg.com/
Net Analytic	www.netanalytic.com
Night Auditors of America	http://www.night-auditors.com/
NIKKEI Research Inc.	http://www.nikkeiresearch.com/
NOP Mystery Shopping	http://www.nopres.co.uk/
North 51st Merchandising Inc.	www.north51.com

Northwest Loss Prevention Consultants (NWLPC)	http://www.nwlpc.com/
Olchak Market Research	http://www.omrdc.com/
On the Sky	http://www.users.qwest.net/ ~brnecksec/
On-Site Solutions, Inc	shoposs@bellsouth.net
Pacific Research Group	http://www.pacificresearchgroup. com/
Palm Scheduling Services	http://palmschedulingservices.com/
Palvelu Plus—Service Plus Oy/Ltd.	jukka.rastas@serviceplus.fi
PAN Research Ltd.	abushnell@panresearch.ie
Pat Henry Perceptions, Inc.	www.thepathenrygroup.com
PatronEdge	http://www.patronedge.com/
People Plus Inc	www.peopleplusinc.net
Performance Edge	http://www.pedge.com/
Person to Person Quality	http://persontopersonquality.com/
Petro Truck Stops	http://www.petrotruckstops.com/
Pinkerton	http://www.pktnshop.com/
Plethora	http://www.benzie.com/ plethora/
Precision Research	http://www.preres.com/
Premier Service Consulting	http://www.premierservice.ca
Premier Mystery Shopping Company, The	www.secretshop.com
Premium Retail Services	www.premiumretail.com
ProDem, Inc.	www.prodem.us
Professional Review	http://www.proreview.com/
Professional Services	www.ps4action.com
Promotion Network, Inc.	http://www.promotionnetworkinc. com/
PROS Professional Review & Operational Shoppes, Inc.	http://www.proreview.com/

Pro-Set, LLC	prosetdavis@charter.net
ProSource Merchandising Service, Inc.	jknox@prosourcemerch.com
Prove of Orlando/Shoppers Critique	http://www.proveoforlando.com/
PulseBack	http://www.pulseback.com/ index2.htm
Quick Test	info@quicktest.com
Quality Assessments Mystery Shoppers	http://www.qams.com/
Quality Assurance Consulting	http://www.qacinc.com/
Quality Check/Under covershoppers	http://www.undercovershoppers. com/
Quality Consultants, Inc.	http://www.qualconsultant.com/
Quality Controlled Services	www.qcs.com
Quality Marketing	http://www.quality-marketing.com
Quality Marketing Group	www.QMGRP.com
Quality Service Inspections (QSI)	http://www.qsispecialists.com/
QualityWorks Associates	http://www.qualityworks.com/
Quest	www.Questservicegroup.com
Quest for Best	http://www.questforbest.com/
RDS, Inc	pattyd@storemind.com
React Surveys	info@reactsurveys.co.uk
Reality Check Mystery Shoppers	http://www.rcmysteryshopper.com/
Report Company	www.logcity.com
Reps Ltd	www.repsltd.com
Resort Loyalty, Inc.	http://www.resortloyalty.com/
Responce Services Corporation	www.responseservices.com
Restaurant Shops Online	www.ranw.com
Retail Biz Consulting	http://www.retailbiz.com/

Retail Evaluators	http://www.retailevaluators.com/
Retail Merchandising Services, Inc.	www.rmservicing.com
Retail Rapport	www.mysteryshopagency.com
Retail Sales Training	http://www.retailsalestrain.com/
Retail Service Evaluations	www.retailserviceevaluatorsinc.com
Retail Services Group, Inc.	www.rsgservices.com
Richey International	www.richeyint.com
Rickie Kruh Research	http://www.rkrmg.com/
Ritter & Associates	http://www.ritterandassociates.com/
Rocky Mountain Merchandising	www.rockymm.com
RoperNOP Mystery Shopping	http://www.cybershoppersonline.com/
RQA, Inc. (Retail Quality Assurance)	http://www.rqa-inc.com/
Sales and Marketing Group	http://www.samgus.com/
Sales Edge	JQuillen@salesedgeservice.com
Satisfaction Services	http://www.satisfactionservicesinc.com/
Scholl Market Research, Inc.	www.imaginusinc.com
Scott Marketing	http://www.scottmktg.com/
Second to None, Inc.	http://www.second-to-none.com/
Secret Shopnet/Service Intelligence	http://www.secretshopnet.com/
Secret Shopper Company	http://www.secretshoppercompany.com/
Select Media Services	lsmith@selectmediaservices.com
Sensors Quality Management/SQM	http://www.sqm.ca/
Service Advantage International (SAI)	http://www.servad.com/
Service Alliance	http://www.serviceallianceinc.com/

Service Dimensions International/Mosaic Group	http://www.mosaicgroupinc.com/
Service Evaluation Concepts	http://www.serviceevaluation.com/
Service Excellence Group	http://www.serviceexcellencegroup.com/
Service Impressions	http://www.serviceimpressions.com/
Service Intelligence	http://www.secretshopnet.com/
Service Perceptions	www.serviceperceptions.com
Service Quality Department	http://www.service-quality.com/
Service Quest	www.myservicequest.com
Service Research	http://expage.com/page/sri
Service Research Corporation	http://serviceresearch.com/
Service Sleuths by Howard Services	http://www.howardservices.com/homess.html
Service Solutions	www.servicesolutionsusa.com
ServiceProbe	http://www.pwgroup.com/sprobe/
ServiceSense	http://www.servicesense.com/
ServiceTRAC	http://www.servicetrac.com/
Ser-View	www.ser-view.com
Set and Service Staffing	www.sasstaffing.com
Service Quality Department	http://www.service-quality.com/index.html
SG Marketing	http://www.sgmarketing.com/
Shop America	http://www.mysteryshopamerica.com/
Shop'n Check	http://www.shopncheck.com/intro.html
Shoppers Critique International	http://www.shopperscritique.com/home.asp
Shopping Detectives, The	www.theshoppingdetectives.com
Sights on Service (Secret Shopper)	http://www.secretshopper.com/

Signature, Inc.	http://www.legendary.net/welcome.htm
Skilcheck Services	http://www.skilcheck.com/
Sneak PeaksMS	www.spbon.com
Solomon Group	http://www.thesolomongroup.com/
Solutions at Work	http://www.solutionsatworkinc.com/
Source One Marketing Group LLC	www.S1marketing.com
Southwest Mystery Shoppers	http://www.mysteryshoppers.com/
SPAR Group	www.sparinc.com
Sparagowski & Associates	http://www.sparagowski.com/
Speedmark Information Services	http://www.speedmarkweb.com/
Spies in Disguise	http://spiesindisguise.com/
Spotchecks Mystery Shopping	http://www.spotchecks.com/
Star Merchandising Service	www.starmerchandising.com
Startex Marketing Services	http://www.startexms.com/
STATOPEX—Canada	http://www.statopex.com/
Store Level Service Group, L.L.C.	www.slsg.net
Storecast Merchandising Corporation	www.storecast.com
Strategic Merchandising Partners	www.smp-inc.com/merchandising
Stratmar Systems, Inc	www.stratmar.com
Sunflower Group, The	www.sunflowergroup.com
Support Financial Resources, Inc.	www.serviceexperiences.com
SurfMerchants	http://www.surfmerchants.com/
Sutter Performance Group	smmyst@aol.com

Systematic Distribution	www.sysdis.com
SystemChec by Orilio & Associates	http://www.systemchec.com/
Taylor Research	http://www.taylorresearch. com/
Tenox Appraisal Systems, Inc.	http://www.weshop4u.com/
TES/RapidCheck	http://www.rapidchek.com/
Testshopper.com	http://testshopper.com/
Texas Shoppers Network	http://www.texasshoppersnetwork. com/
TheServiceTeam.com	www.theserviceteam.com
THINKSMART	http://www.thinksmart.es/
TNS	http://www.tns-i.com/
Trend Source	http://www.trendsource.com/
TRS Merchandising	www.trsmerchandising. com
Ultra Shopper	bkonners@mindspring. com
Vantage Points	http://www.vantagepointsonline. com/
Video Eyes	http://www.videoeyes.net/
VIM	www.vim-inc.com
VIP Sales & Merchandising, Inc.	vipsales@alltel.net
Wal-Mart	http://www.walmart.com/cservice/ ca_research.gsp?NavMode=8
Waveland Group, The	http://www.thewavelandgroup. com/
WebbTech Data Services	www.webbtech.com
Williams & Associates, Inc., of Tennessee	www.williamsassociates.net/visual
Wynn & Associates, Inc.	ewynn@flash.net

Minimizing the Search

One commonly asked question is, how can I limit my search to a specific focus, such as companies that mystery-shop hotels in the state of Arizona. The MSPA is the Mystery Shopper Providers Association and is an organization of mystery-shopping companies for mystery-shopping companies. It mainly offers assistance to companies, however, there is a wonderful component on the web site which allows a shopper to search for companies by industry, country, or state. For example, if I wanted to shop hotels in California, I could run a search by Hotels in the state of California and it would provide a listing of every mystery-shopping company that has hotel accounts in the state of California.

MSPA www.mysteryshop.org

Companies Not Requiring Computer Access

I have included a list of over 100 companies that do not require the shopper to have computer access. The methods you may use to contact these companies are phone, fax, and snail mail (regular U.S. Postal Service). Some of the companies do indeed have an email address listed, and if you have computer access you should email your letter of intent. However, it is not necessary to have a computer to succeed as a shopper.

To save both time and money, I recommend that you contact the companies in this order. First, call all the 800 numbers and inquire about the need for shoppers in the areas you frequent regularly and periodically. Remember, these are mystery-shopping companies, and they are expecting your call. They will not be surprised or disoriented when you call, so have no fear.

Next, fax your letter of intent to all the 800 fax numbers, and then to the long distance fax numbers. The purchase of a fax is the one investment that I highly recommend you make, for you will be able to receive and send reports and it will double as a copy machine. This is important because you will be asked to mail out your original receipts, and you will need to make copies of all your information for tax purposes, or to send to the company if it does not receive your original information.

Finally, the last method is snail mail (regular U.S. Postal Service). This is by far the most expensive method, for you must pay for postage, envelopes, paper, and printing.

A common question I receive is, what happens when there are no companies in my local area? Please keep in mind that it is typical for one company to serve a national account. That company may not be located in your city, but it will certainly need shoppers in your city. For example, a company in Florida mystery-shops Kmart on a national level. Although it is not located, in say, California, it has a national contract, and it will need shoppers to visit the Kmart locations in California. In addition, if you travel out of state, you may want to pick up a hotel assignment on your next vacation, so that all your expenses are part of a business trip. This will be discussed in detail in Chapter 8.

Here is a list of mystery-shopping companies that do not utilize the Internet as the primary method of communication. You can contact these by mail with a letter of interest, by phone, email, or fax; or as noted in the comments.

Accurate Data Marketing, Inc.

1247 Milwaukee Ave., Suite 200

Glenview, IL 60025

Phone: (847) 390-7777

Fax: (847) 390-7849

Email: AcurData@aol.com

ALCOPS

6701 W. 64th St., Suite 221

Shawnee Mission, KS 66202-4170

Phone: (913) 362-0104 or (800)345-7347

Applied Research West

Phone: (562) 493-1079

Barry Leeds & Associates, Inc.

38 E. 29th Street

New York, NY 10016

Phone: (212) 889-5941

Fax: (212) 889-6066

Email: bleedsny@aol.com

Web site: www.barryleedsassoc.com

Beyond Hello

6225 University Ave.

P.O. Box 5240

Madison, WI 53705-5240

Phone: (800) 321-2588 or (608) 232-1414

Fax: (800) 868-5203

Beyond Marketing Group Inc.

P. O. Box 11344

Winston-Salem, NC 27116

Fax: (336) 924-0062

Email: bmg@bellsouth.net

The Blackstone Group

360 N. Michigan Ave., Suite 1500

Chicago, IL 60601

Phone: (312) 419-0400

Fax: (312) 419-8419

Business Resources

2222 Western Trails Blvd.

Austin, TX 78745-1601

Capstone Research, Inc.

623 Ridge Rd.

Lyndhurst, NJ 07071

Phone: (201) 939-0600

Fax: (201) 939-3037

Email: info@capstoneresearch.com

Carol Max Marketing Services, Inc.
P.O. Box 41127
St. Louis, MO 63141
Phone: (314) 434-2157
Fax: (314) 434-2890
Email: 73003.1722@compuserve.com
Prefers that you contact via email to see if there are jobs available
in your area.

C.B. DuPree Associates
299 Highbridge St.
Fayetteville, NY 13066
Phone: (315) 637-2321
Fax: (315) 637-2122
Please send letter of intent to apply.

Certified Reports
7 Hudson St.
P.O. Box 447
Kinderhook, NY 12106-0447
Phone: (518) 758-6403
Fax: (518) 758-6451 or (518) 758-6459

Chesapeake Surveys
4 Park Center Court, Suite 1004
Owing Mills, MD 21117
Phone: (410) 356-3566
Fax: (410) 581-6700

Commercial Service Systems (C.S.S.)
6946 Van Nuys Blvd.
Van Nuys, CA 91405-3963
Phone: (800) 898-9021
(818) or (626) 997-7955

Compass Marketing Research
3725 DaVinci Court, Suite 100
Norcross, GA 30092
Phone: (770) 448-0754
Fax: (770) 416-7586
Email: cmrcompass@aol.com
Metro area: Atlanta, Georgia

Confero
120 Edinburgh Dr.
Cary, NC 27511-6434
Phone: (800) 477-3947 or (919) 469-5200

Consumer Critique, Inc.
15100 SE 38th St.
Suite #761
Bellevue, WA 98006

Consumer Impressions, Inc.
P.O. Box 866996
Plano, TX 75086-6996
Phone: (800) 747-1838 or (800) 336-0159
Fax: (800) 645-5552
Texas, Oklahoma, Kansas, Missouri, Illinois, and Colorado only.

Consumer Pulse
725 South Adams Rd., Suite 265
Birmingham, MI 48009
Phone: (810) 540-5330
Send letter of intent.

Critique International
120 E. 5th Ave.
Windermere, FL 34786

(407) 876-1333

Web site: http://home.att.net/~AGrimpe/

Use address above for letter of Intent.

No phone calls, please.

Cross Financial Group

2418 Ammon Ave., Suite 100

Lincoln, NE 68507

Phone: (800) 566-3491

Fax: (402) 441-3136

Email: crossfin@aol.com

CSI

Route 9, Box 447

Kinderhook, NY 12106

Customer Perspectives

213 West River Rd.

Hooksett, NH 03106-2628

Phone: (603) 647-1300 or (800) 277-4677

Fax: (603) 647-0900

Fax letter of intent.

Customer Point-of-View

68-100 Ramon Rd., Suite B-10

Cathedral City, CA 92234

Phone: (760) 324-9270

Customerize Consulting

9921 Carmel Mountain Rd., #185

San Diego, CA 92129

(800) 330-5948

Fax: (619) 689 9004

Email: glscheid@cts.com

D.S.G.

2110 East 1st St., Suite 106

Santa Ana, CA 92705

Phone: (800) 290-3503

Email: DSGER@worldnet.att.net

Send letter of intent.

Datazones (VALICO)

P.O. Box 1949

Valrico, FL 33395

Email: infomation@datazones.com

Web site: http://www.datazones.com

To apply: http://www.datazones.com/mysteryshopping/apply.html

David Sparks and Associates

Phone: (800) 849-7467

Email: dsa@sparksresearch.com

DCW Interviewing Service

2313 Ashdown Dr.

Bossier City, LA 71111-5917

Phone: (318) 742-0126

Fax: (318) 741-3071

Metro area: Shreveport, Louisiana

Ehrhart-Babie/NRTI

14 Industrial Ave.

Mahwah, NJ 07430

Phone: (201) 934-0600

Fax: (201) 934-3935

EKEI Enterprises

P.O. Box 153773

Irving, TX 75050

Phone: (972) 790-7214
Fax: (972) 513-0138
Email: EKEI@msn.com or Ekroussaki@aol.com
Contact Elsie Kroussaki.

Focus Groups of Cleveland Survey Center
2 Summit Park Dr., Suite 225
Cleveland, OH 44131
Phone: (216) 642-8883 or (800) 950-9010
Fax: (216) 642-8876
Metro area: Cleveland, Ohio

Frances Bauman Associates
23 Girard Street
Marlboro, NJ 07746
Phone: (908) 536-9712
Fax: (908) 536-3256

Galli Research Services
3728 Bernard St.
Chicago, IL 60618
Phone: (773) 4-SURVEY
Fax: (773) 478-7899

Gourmet Club
Web site: http://www.gourmetclub.com/htmlast/qst.htm

Greater Pittsburgh Research Services
5950 Steubenville Pike
Pittsburgh, PA 15136
Phone: (412) 788-4570
Fax: (412) 788-4582

Gulf State Research Center
Bon Marche Mall

7361 Florida Blvd.

Baton Rouge, LA 70806

Phone: (504) 926-3827 or (800) 848-2555

Fax: (504) 925-9990

Highsmith-Charnock Interviewing Service, Inc.

2912 Sussex Rd.

Augusta, GA 30909-3532

Email: ResearchGA@computer1.net

Houston Consumer Research

730 Almeda Mall

Houston, TX 77075-3514

Phone: (713) 944-1431

Fax: (713) 944-3527

Metro area: Houston, Texas

Hyland B. Company

Corporate Office

4647 North 32nd St., Suite B-190

Phoenix, AZ 85018

Phone: (602) 381-1177 or (800) 382-1177

Fax: (602) 381-1024

Hyland B. Company

Texas & Southern Region

2301 Ohio Dr., Suite 130

Plano, TX 75093

Phone: (214) 964-7669

Fax: (214) 612-8230

Hyland B. Company

California & Western Region

35226 Faraday Court

Fremont, CA 94536
Phone: (510) 796-7590
Fax: (510) 796-7590

IMAGES Market Research
17118 Peachtree Rd., Suite 650
Atlanta, GA 30309
Phone: (404) 892-2931
Fax: (404) 892-8651
Email: IMAGESUSA@aol.com
Metro area: Atlanta, Georgia

In Gold Research Services, Inc.
17501 Janesville Rd.
Muskego, WI 53150
Phone: (414) 679-2600
Fax: (414) 679-1445

Infinite Wisdom
Oceanside, CA 92056
Phone: (619) 758-8578
Fax: (619) 758-8578

Infotel
P.O. Box 1000
Los Gatos, CA 95031
Phone: (800) 876-1110
Send letter of intent.

Integrated Research Associates, Inc.
708 Walnut Ave., Suite 800
Cincinnati, OH 45202
Phone: (513) 361-2700
Email: iresearcha@aol.com

Metro area: Cincinnati, Ohio

Interviewing Service of America
16005 Sherman Way, Suite 209
Van Nuys, CA 91405
Phone: (818) or (626) 989-1044
Fax: (818) or (626) 782-1309

Irwin Research Services
9250 Baymeadows Rd., Suite 350
Jacksonville, FL 32256
Phone: (904) 731-1811
Fax: (904) 731-1225

Isaacson Group
885 Forester St.
San Francisco, CA 94127-2307
Phone: (415) 585-9729
Fax: (415) 585-8736
Email: i6ngrp@aol.com
Send letter of intent and résumé.

Issues and Answers Network, Inc.
5151 Bonney Rd.
Virginia Beach, VA 23462
Phone: (757) 456-1100
Fax: (757) 456-0377
Email: info@issans.com

J.M. Ridgeway, Inc.
P.O. Box 875
Los Altos, CA 94023
Phone: (650) 984-1623 or (800) 367-7434

Jordan Associates
P.O. Box 1100
Garden Grove, CA 92842
Phone: (714) 520-0900

L.A. Research, Inc.
9010 Reseda Blvd., Suite 109
Northridge, CA 91324-3921
Phone: (818) 993-6440
Fax: (818) 993-5664
Metro area: Los Angeles, California
Call or write to apply.

Lenux Research/Mystery Guest, Inc.
668 N. Orlando Ave., Suite 107
Maitland, FL 32751
Phone: (407) 647-3333
Fax: (407) 647-3016

Main Resources Services
P.O. Box 220
North Plains, OR 97133-0220
Phone: (800) 559-6662
Fax: (503) 647-5813
Send letter of intent.

Marcomm Group
5 Mount Royal Ave.
Marlborough, MA 01752-1981
Phone: (508) 481-3290 or (800) 370-8300

MBA, Inc.
407 Wekiva Springs Rd., Suite 213

Longwood, FL 32779
Phone: (407) 682-9400
Fax: (407) 323-5217
Email: mba@iag.net

Mercantile Systems
Email: Sheath5399@aol.com

Meyers Research Center
58 W. 40th St.
New York, NY 10018
Phone: (212) 391-0166
Fax: (212) 768-0268
Email: MRC00@aol.com
Contact by mail.
Contact Michele Steigerwald.

Midwest Survey & Marketing
8922 Cuming St.
Omaha, NE 68114-2732
Phone: (402) 392-0755
Fax: (402) 392-1068

MPS Research, Inc.
16-00 Route 208
Fair Lawn, NJ 07410
Phone: (201) 703-6868
Fax: (201) 703-6870
Email: MPSResrch@aol.com

Mystery Guest, Inc.
2107 Park Ave. N.

Winter Park, FL 32789
Phone: (407) 647-3333
Fax: (407) 647-3016

Mystery Shopper Inc.
3311 Mercer St.
Houston, TX 77027-6019

Mystery Shopper USA
Sarasota, FL
Phone: (941) 379-5611
Countrywide
Takes applications over phone.

Mystery Shoppers
5308 Turtle Point Ln.
Knoxville, TX 37919-9339
Phone: (423) 450-8841
Fax: (423) 450-8839

Mystery Shoppers Anonymous
1712 W. Spring Creek Pkwy.
Plano, TX 75023-4305
Phone: (800) 847-1934

Mystery Shoppers Inc./Trendsource
620 State St., Suite 225
San Diego, CA 92101
Phone: (619) 239-2543 or (619) 595-4131
www.trendsource.com for applications

Mystery Shoppers Inc.
6300 Richmond Ave., Suite 208
Houston, TX 77057-5927

Mystery Shopping Inc.
11431 N. Port Washington Rd.
Mequon, WI 53092-3449
Phone: (414) 241-5262

Mystic Marketing
6654 Mohawk Court
Columbia, MD 21046
Phone: (301) 596-1437

National Market Research
Attn: Research
P.O. Box 16757
Stamford, CT 06905
Fax: (203) 322-5848
Mail résumé or background letter of intent.

New South Research
3000 Riverchase, Suite 405
Birmingham, AL 35244
Phone: (205) 985-3344
Fax: (205) 985-3346
Email: NSRJJ@aol.com

Opinions of Sacramento
2025 Hurley Way, Suite 110
Sacramento, CA 95825
Phone: (916) 568-1226
Fax: (916) 568-6725
Email: opinionsos@aol.com
Focus groups metro area: Sacramento, California

Pat Henry Market Research, Inc.
230 Huron Rd. N.W., Suite 10043

Cleveland, OH 44113

Phone: (216) 621-3831

Fax: (216) 621-8455

Email: phenry3@ix.netcom.com

Metro area: Cleveland, Ohio

Peak Performance

P.O. Box 177767

Irving, TX 75017-7767

Phone: (800) 326-4018 or 972-259-1778

Email: GMAW10191@aol.com

Call if you live in: South Dakota, Nebraska, Minnesota, Iowa, Indiana, Illinois, Wisconsin, or Michigan.

Perceptive Market Research, Inc.

2306 S.W. 13th St., Suite 807

Gainesville, FL 32608

Phone: (800) 749-6760 or (352) 336-6760

Fax: (352) 336-6763

Email: surveys@pmrresearch.com

Polly Graham & Associates, Inc.

3000 Riverchase Galleria, Suite 310

Birmingham, AL 35244-2344

Phone: (205) 985-3099

Fax: (205) 985-3066

Metro area: Birmingham, Alabama

Prove of Orlando

Phone: (800) 326-4399

Quality Assessments Mystery Shoppers, Inc.

P.O. Box 9009

Austin, TX 78766-9009

Phone: (512) 263-3388

Fax: (512) 263-3338

Email: bonniecnr@aol.com

Quality Performance Group

Chesapeake, VA

Phone: 803-420-0383 or 800-269-0383

Fax: 803-420-2558

Email: qpgquality@aol.com

The Question Shop, Inc.

2860 N. Santiago Blvd., Suite 100

Orange, CA 92667

Phone: (714) 974-8020 or (800) 411-7550

Fax: (714) 974-6968

Metro area: Orange County, California

Quality Assessments Mystery Shoppers

P.O. Box 9009

Austin, TX 78766-9009

Phone: (512)263-3388

Fax: (512) 263-3338

Quest Marketing Group

400 Clifton Corp. Pkwy., Suite 472

Clifton Park, NY 12065-3839

Phone: (518)373-1990

Fax: (518) 373-4824

Research House, Inc.

1867 Yonge St., 2nd Floor

Toronto, Ontario, Canada

M4S 1Y5

Phone: (416) 488-2333

Fax: (416) 488-2391
Email: mail@research-house.ca
Metro area: Toronto, Ontario

RKR/Rickie Kruh Research
2138 South Bay Ln.
Reston, VA 22091
Phone: (703) 476-4444

Rossow Interviewing
2713 15th Ave. N.
Fort Dodge, IA 50501
Phone: (515) 576-6464
Fax: (515) 576-5454
Metro area: Fort Dodge, Iowa

Satisfaction Services
Phone: (888) 667-8811 or (800) 564-6574
Email: www.jjmurski@erols.com

Savitz Research Center, Inc.
13747 Montfort Dr., Suite 111
Dallas, TX 75240
Phone: (972) 386-4050
Fax: (972) 450-2507
Metro area: Dallas/Ft. Worth, Texas

Schlesinger Associates, Inc.
1 Academy St.
Princeton, NJ 08540-9590
Phone: (609) 924-1818
Email: sasmktres@aol.com
Metro area: Northern New Jersey

Service Evaluation Concepts

P.O. Box 9202

Old Bethpage, NY 11804-9863

Phone: (800) 695-4746

(800) 732-4748

Fax: (516) 576-1195

United States & Canada

The company would like you to apply by phone. Speak slowly and
clearly to the 800 number.

Or send a letter of intent, with an index card including your name,
address, and telephone number, along with a self-addressed
stamped envelope.

Service Excellence Group

211 Stablestone Dr.

St. Louis, MO 63017

Phonc: (800) 888-9189

Fax: (314) 878-1818

Email: servicex@aol.com

Service Excellence Group (Segova)

2415 N. Dearing St.

Alexandria, VA 22302

Phone: 703-379-9877

Email: Segova@aol.com

Service Research Corp.

6201 S. 58th St., Suite A

Lincoln, NE 68516-3678

Phone: (402) 434-5000

Email: srcbritt@aol.com

Service Track

Phone: (800) 224-6875

Shoneys, Inc
1835 Union Ave.
Nashville TN 38104-3942
Phone: (800) 626-5630 or 615-391-5201
Fax: (615) 231-2604
Email: wrightah@shoneys.com

Shop N Chek
Phone: (800) 669-6526
Web site: www.shopnchek.com

Shoppers View
960 Scribner Ave., N.W.
Grand Rapids, MI 49504
Phone: (616) 356-2588 or (800) 264-5677
Fax: (616) 356-2589
Email: mystshop@aol.com

Shopping for Performance
10700 Richmond, Suite 100
Houston, TX 77042-4905
Phone: (713) 953-9530
Fax: (713) 953-9870

Send a cover letter and let the company know the areas you are
available to shop in.

Survey Service, Inc.
1911 Sheridan Dr.
Buffalo, NY 14223
Phone: (716) 876-6450
Fax: (716) 876-0430
Email: sservice@surveyservice.com
Metro area: Buffalo, New York

Surveys Unlimited, Inc.

232 Vincent Dr.

East Meadows, NY 11554

Phone: (516) 794-5650

Fax: (516) 794-3841

Email: nysurveys@aol.com

Metro area: New York City, New York

System Check

10225 Barnes Canyon Rd., Suite A200,

San Diego, CA 92121

Phone: (619) 546-0072 or (800) 228-9244

Web site: www.systemchec.com for applications

Wolf/Altschul/Callahan, Inc.

60 Madison Ave., 5th floor

New York, NY 10010-1600

Phone: (212) 725-8840

Fax: (212) 213-9247

Email: jimfrisch@aol.com

Remember, the first few months are the initial start-up period, and in order to succeed, you must apply, apply, apply. Here is another commonly asked question:

Dear Dr. Newhouse,
    It has been quite some time, and I have not received an assignment. I got a call the other day for an assignment in Tucson, which is 2 hours away. Should I take it?
    Please help.
    Sandy

* * * *

Dear Sandy,
    The first question I have is, how many companies have you applied to? If you rely on the message boards only as your main

source of acquiring assignments, you are going to wait a long time. However, if you apply to a couple of hundred agencies, your phone will ring off the hook! Here's the main idea: Suppose you were hunting for a full-time job and you sent out only10 résumés and no one responded. Does this mean no one is hiring? The key to being a successful shopper is apply, apply, apply.

Next, a rule of thumb is to never drive more than 20 minutes from your home for a mystery shop unless you were going there anyway. If you drive hours for a few dollars, you will barely make minimum wage and will quickly get burned out.

Finally, I would encourage you to acquire some type of additional mystery-shopping training, such as attending a seminar in person or online or perhaps purchasing a book.

Reports

There are basically four types of reports that you will encounter as a mystery shopper: simple yes or no, full narrative, rating scale, or a combination of all three. Most reports are a combination of all three; however, several of the easy assignments for beginning shoppers, are assignments such as gas stations or fast food, which use simple yes or no reports. In this section we will discuss and review each type of report.

Simple Yes or No

As stated, an assignment requiring only a simple yes or no form is the most basic type of assignment as well as the easiest, to do, easiest to acquire, and fastest to complete. Assignment fees typically range from $6 to $50, but are typically an average of $10. The form has simple questions such as what was the employee's name, did the employee smile, did you receive everything you ordered, and was your food hot, fresh, and tasty.

Full Narrative

An assignment requiring a full narrative is by far the most complicated type of assignment as well as the most difficult to acquire and complete. Required narratives can range from one paragraph to over 500 pages long, and fees range from $10 to $3,000, with an average of $150. The narrative is used to describe in detail all occurrences and interactions in the business establishment. The experience of completing a high-end assignment of this nature is equivalent to giving birth. These assignments are designed for the experienced shopper, and I would highly recommend that you not accept this type of assignment until you have at least 50 simple assignments under your belt.

Rating Scale

These assignments are few and far between and are mostly completed on the Internet. You will be asked to rate the level of service, cleanliness, food quality, and so on, on a scale of 1 to 10 with 10 usually being the best. The company will provide a guideline for what is considered a 10 as well as ask you to compare fine dining to fine dining and fast food to fast food. These assignments typically pay from $10 to $120, with an average of $15.

Combination

The final category includes the majority of mystery-shopping assignments. It is the most common and is moderately easy to acquire with a minimal amount of experience. The pay range is typically from $10 to $150, with an average of about $30 to 40. An example of this type of assignment is a visit to an apartment complex. The shopper is asked to answer simple yes or no questions about the cleanliness of the property or if he or she received a greeting from the property agent. Next, the shopper is asked to rate the agent's overall sales ability on a scale, and finally the shopper is asked to write a five-paragraph narrative covering the telephone conversation, the greeting, the tour, closing the sale, and the overall condition of the property.

The next few pages give an example of a typical report that you may encounter and also an example of a completed form.

Sonya's Mystery Shoppers

P.O. Box 706
Omaha, NE 68010

sonyasmysteryshoppers@home.com
(402) 555-1212

J'S BAR & GRILL
14471 Sahler Plaza
Beverly Hills, CA 90210

Shopper Name: _____   Date: _____

Shopper ID: _____   Time Entered: _____

                                                      Time Exited: _____

Transaction # (from receipt): _____   Amount of Tip left: _____

Total Amount of Check: _____   Misc. Expenses (parking, etc.) _____ -

PHONE CALL   Name: _____ (if none given, note male/female)

1. Time call was made: _____

2. Number of rings before phone was answered: _____

3. Did the person identify the location and state their name?   YES _____   NO _____

4. Were they polite and easily understood?   YES _____   NO _____

5. Based on the phone conversation, would you dine at this location?   YES _____   NO _____

COMMENTS: (please explain all "NO" answers)

HOST/HOSTESS   Name/Description: _____

6. Were you greeted within 30 seconds upon entering the location?   YES _____   NO _____

    If No, how many seconds: _____

7. Were you asked for a smoking preference?   YES _____   NO _____

8. Did the seater walk you to your table at a comfortable pace?   YES _____   NO _____

9. Were children given special attention?   N/A _____   YES _____   NO _____

10. Did the seater extend a greeting such as "Enjoy your meal" before walking away?   YES _____   NO _____

COMMENTS: (please explain all "NO" answers)

SERVER/BARTENDER   Name/Description: _____

11. Were you greeted within 2 minutes of being seated?   YES _____   NO _____

    If No, how many minutes? _____

12. Did the server offer you a specific beverage?   YES _____   NO _____

    If Yes, what was offered? _____

13. Did the server offer you a specific appetizer?   YES _____   NO _____

    If Yes, what was offered? _____

14. Was the server knowledgeable of menu items?   YES _____   NO_____

      What was asked: _____

      What was said: _____

15. Did the server notify you of the daily specials?   YES _____   NO_____

16. Was the server genuinely friendly and attentive?   YES _____   NO_____

17. Did the server make you feel welcome?   YES _____   NO_____

18. Based on the service received, would you return to this location?   YES _____   NO_____

COMMENTS: (please explain all "NO" answers)

MANAGEMENT   **Name/Description:** _____

19. Was the manager interacting with and available to the staff?   YES _____   NO_____

20. Was the manager well groomed and appropriately dressed?   YES _____   NO_____

21. Did you receive a table visit?   YES _____   NO_____

22. If there was a problem, was it handled efficiently and to your satisfaction?

                                     N/A _____   YES _____   NO_____

MAINTENANCE

23. Was the exterior well maintained and free from unnecessary debris?   YES _____   NO_____

24. Were the sidewalks well lit with no more than two bulbs not working?   YES _____   NO_____

25. Was the interior tile/carpet clean and well maintained?   YES _____   NO_____

26. Were the tables and utensils clean and free from spots?   YES _____   NO_____

27. Were the tables/chairs in good repair?   YES _____   NO_____

COMMENTS: (please explain all "NO" answers)

FOOD ITEMS

First entrée ordered: _____   Second entrée ordered: _____

	YES	NO		YES	NO
Was the entrée attractively arranged?	_____	_____	Was the entrée attractively arranged?	_____	_____
Served at the correct temperatures?	_____	_____	Served at the correct temperatures?	_____	_____
Prepared as ordered?	_____	_____	Prepared as ordered?	_____	_____
Did the entrée have a good flavour?	_____	_____	Did the entrée have a good flavour?	_____	_____
Were the portion sizes adequate?	_____	_____	Were the portion sizes adequate?	_____	_____
Did you feel the entrée was a good value?	_____	_____	Did you feel the entrée was a good value?	_____	_____
Would you order this item again?	_____	_____	Would you order this item again?	_____	_____

Beverage Order : _____

Appetizer Order : _____

Dessert Order : _____

COMMENTS: (please explain all "NO" answers)

TIMING

Time Beverage Ordered: _____	Beverage Delivered: _____
Time Appetizer Ordered: _____	Appetizer Delivered: _____
Time Entrée's Ordered: _____	Last Entrée Delivered: _____
Time of server check back: _____	Time of manager visit: _____
Time Dessert Ordered: _____	Dessert Delivered: _____
Time of check delivery: _____	Time of check pickup: _____

OVERALL SATISFACTION

28. Based on this visit, would you return to this location?   YES _____   NO _____

29. Based on this visit, would you recommend this location to your friends?   YES _____   NO _____

COMMENTS: (please explain all "NO" answers)

Sonya's Mystery Shoppers

P.O. Box 706
Omaha, NE 68010

sonyasmysteryshoppers@home.com
(402) 555-1212

J'S BAR & GRILL
14471 Sahler Plaza
Beverly Hills, CA 90210

Shopper Name: Bryan Grafft	Date:	7/10/2001
Shopper ID: 950723	Time Entered:	6:53 PM
	Time Exited:	7:59 PM
Transaction # (from receipt): 035478	Amount of Tip left:	$7.00
Total Amount of Check: $45.38	Misc. Expenses (parking, etc.)	$ -

PHONE CALL   Name: Carrie   (if none given, note male/female)

1. Time call was made: 6:15 PM

2. Number of rings before phone was answered: 2

3. Did the person identify the location and state their name?   YES X   NO

4. Were they polite and easily understood?   YES X   NO

5. Based on the phone conversation, would you dine at this location?   YES X   NO

COMMENTS: (please explain all "NO" answers)

Carrie was very friendly and outgoing. She gave clear and accurate directions to the location. When asked, she was able to give me the hours of operation. Carrie cheerfully invited me to the restaurant. Our phone conversation would have motivated me to dine there, had I not been sure of which restaurant to dine at. My overall first impression was favorable at this point.

HOST/HOSTESS   Name/Description: Aaron, male, 6'4"-6'6", short straight brown hair, 20-25 years.

6. Were you greeted within 30 seconds upon entering the location?   YES X   NO

    If No, how many seconds:

7. Were you asked for a smoking preference?   YES X   NO

8. Did the seater walk you to your table at a comfortable pace?   YES X   NO

9. Were children given special attention?   N/A X   YES   NO

10. Did the seater extend a greeting such as "Enjoy your meal" before walking away?   YES X   NO

COMMENTS: (please explain all "NO" answers)

Aaron greeted us immediately upon entering the location. We were asked if we had a smoking preference. Aaron was very personable and chatted with us while walking us to the table at a comfortable pace. He made sure the table was satisfactory and let us know the server would be with us shortly. We did not have children in our party; however, we noticed the children in the restaurant were given crayons and paper to keep them busy.

SERVER/BARTENDER   Name/Description: Melissa, female, 5'7"-5'9", long curly blonde hair, 20-23

11. Were you greeted within 2 minutes of being seated?   YES   NO X

    If No, how many minutes?   3.5 minutes

12. Did the server offer you a specific beverage?   YES X   NO

    If Yes, what was offered?   Coke or Iced Tea

13. Did the server offer you a specific appetizer?   YES X   NO

    If Yes, what was offered?   Cheese Fries or Buffalo Wings

14. Was the server knowledgeable of menu items?   YES __X__   NO _____

       What was asked: Was the Spinach Dip made fresh onsite, or was it received prepared.

       What was said: The cooks make it fresh from scratch.

15. Did the server notify you of the daily specials?   YES _____   NO __X__

16. Was the server genuinely friendly and attentive?   YES __X__   NO _____

17. Did the server make you feel welcome?   YES __X__   NO _____

18. Based on the service received, would you return to this location?   YES __X__   NO _____

COMMENTS: (please explain all "NO" answers)

The location was very busy, so we were not greeted within two minutes; however, we felt the wait time was appropriate given the situation. Our server was knowledgeable of menu items and seemed confident and comfortable with her answers. She was very attentive and made herself available to the guests in her section. Our server did not mention the daily specials, but did use suggestive selling techniques. She attempted to upgrade our entree order by adding a salad bar. We felt we were valued as customers and will surely return!

MANAGEMENT   **Name/Description:**   Chris, male, 5'8"-5'10", short black hair, 30's, wearing glasses.

19. Was the manager interacting with and available to the staff?   YES __X__   NO _____

20. Was the manager well groomed and appropriately dressed?   YES __X__   NO _____

21. Did you receive a table visit?   YES _____   NO __X__

22. If there was a problem, was it handled efficiently and to your satisfaction?   N/A __X__   YES _____   NO _____

MAINTENANCE

23. Was the exterior well maintained and free from unnecessary debris?   YES __X__   NO _____

24. Were the sidewalks well lit with no more than two bulbs not working?   YES __X__   NO _____

25. Was the interior tile/carpet clean and well maintained?   YES __X__   NO _____

26. Were the tables and utensils clean and free from spots?   YES __X__   NO _____

27. Were the tables/chairs in good repair?   YES __X__   NO _____

COMMENTS: (please explain all "NO" answers)

The manager was observed interacting with the staff and the customers in the location. Although we did not specifically receive a table visit, the manager was seen stopping at several tables around us. The location was about 95% full, and the manager was busy assisting the servers and bussing tables. The interior and exterior of the location were well maintained throughout our visit. The tables and chairs were in good repair with no visible flaws.

FOOD ITEMS

First entrée ordered: Chicken Tender Platter   Second entrée ordered: 8oz. Ribeye Dinner

	YES	NO		YES	NO
Was the entree attractively arranged?	X		Was the entrée attractively arranged?	X	
Served at the correct temperatures?	X		Served at the correct temperatures?	X	
Prepared as ordered?	X		Prepared as ordered?		X
Did the entrée have a good flavour?	X		Did the entrée have a good flavour?	X	
Were the portion sizes adequate?	X		Were the portion sizes adequate?	X	
Did you feel the entrée was a good value?	X		Did you feel the entrée was a good value?	X	
Would you order this item again?	X		Would you order this item again?	X	

Beverage Order :   Iced Tea, Sprite

Appetizer Order :   Spinach Dip

Dessert Order :   Ice Cream Brownie Sundae

COMMENTS: (please explain all "NO" answers)

The entrée's were attractively arranged and served at the appropriate temperatures. The Ribeye was asked to be prepared Medium Well, and was served Well Done. Both entrée's had excellent flavor and the portion sizes of both exceeded our expectations. We felt the entrée's were a good value for the price.

TIMING

Time Beverage Ordered:	6:56 PM	Beverage Delivered:	6:59 PM
Time Appetizer Ordered:	6:59 PM	Appetizer Delivered:	7:11 PM
Time Entrée's Ordered:	7:02 PM	Last Entrée Delivered:	7:23 PM
Time of server check back:	7:25 PM	Time of manager visit:	00:00 PM
Time Dessert Ordered:	7:44 PM	Dessert Delivered:	7:46 PM
Time of check delivery:	7:52 PM	Time of check pickup:	7:54 PM

OVERALL SATISFACTION

28. Based on this visit, would you return to this location?   YES   X   NO _____

29. Based on this visit, would you recommend this location to your friends?   YES   X   NO _____

COMMENTS: (please explain all "NO" answers)

The food at this location is excellent! We received terrific service from our server. All of the employees we came into contact with were very polite and seemed to genuinely enjoy serving others. Given the full capacity of the location, we were extremely impressed with the service speed and food delivery! We were very impressed by the hostess. The hostess stand was near the salad bar. A customer dropped one of the serving utensils on the floor and put it back on the counter. The employee immediately removed the utensil and replaced it with a clean one. We are looking forward to returning to this location and will most definitely refer our friends! Thank you!

An Assignment,
Now What?

There are several methods by which a company may contact you. You may open your mailbox one day and find an assignment with instructions. Next, you may receive a phone call from a scheduler stating that there is an assignment in your area and asking if you are interested. You may receive an email notice of assignments in your area or a notice that assignments have been posted to a web site for your selection. Finally, you may visit a web site and assign yourself to a location. Regardless of how you acquire your first assignment, you will be nervous and excited at the same time. However, there are several factors that you should consider when accepting your first assignment.

Instructions

Instructions are the most important component of the assignment for if you make a crucial error, you may not be paid. You may be given specific instructions such as, do not order the lobster dinner for two or you will not be paid. In addition, you will be asked for the employee's name, and if you do not get it, you will not be paid. Be sure to read the instructions carefully and familiarize yourself with the survey form before you visit the location. There should be no doubt in your mind as to what you are to evaluate. Finally, several mystery-shopping companies may ask you to complete a test in order to evaluate your comprehension or may review a training module with you via telephone. Make sure you are prepared.

Travel

You will not receive the exact assignment location until you request it. You may want to ask for this information and look up the location at www.yahoo.com or www.mapquest.com before agreeing to accept the assignment. I was once offered an assignment in Phoenix, only to find out that it was actually located in Anthem Way, which is a community 45 miles away. Phoenix is a large metropolitan city, and an assignment can be anywhere from 5 miles to 50 miles away. A $10 assignment in a distant community is not really worth the travel time unless you were going to go there anyway.

Another precaution worth mentioning is to verify the actual location address to be sure you are at the right place. My girlfriend Kathleen was once assigned a restaurant on a street that had three restaurants with the same name, and she went to the wrong location. She was not paid or reimbursed, and she opted never to mystery-shop again. This is a really important issue, especially with grocery store mergers. In the area where I live, there are two stores of the same grocery chain across the street from each other, but they are listed as being in different cities. So be sure to verify the location address on the building if there is any doubt in your mind.

Time and Date Constraints

The time and date constraints consist of the time and date when the shop is to be performed and the due date of the assignment. It is important that you are able to visit the location on the specified date and complete the evaluation on time.

Each company has a different requirement for when assignments are to be completed. One company may have the parameters of any time during the month of October, and another company may want you to visit a restaurant this Tuesday between 11:00 a.m. and 2:00 p.m. for lunch. Therefore, if you work full-time and it is impossible for you to have lunch across town on Tuesday, you should humbly decline the assignment and ask about evening or weekend opportunities.

The next parameter is the due date. The due date is typically some period of time after the completion of the assignment. It may be anywhere from 2 to 72 hours. Most assignments are due within 24 hours of the completion of the assignment. For example, if you visit a restaurant on Tuesday at 6:00 p.m. and the report is due within 24 hours, you must submit the assignment by 6:00 p.m. the following day. Some companies may deduct a portion of the payment if the assignment is submitted late or if it is incomplete.

My girlfriend Elaine ran into a payment problem because of this issue. The assignment clearly stated that the report was to be submitted within 48 hours of the visit. She had visited a national eyewear store and was to receive a payment for the visit as well as a 50 percent refund if she opted to purchase a pair of glasses. Well, she completed the visit, purchased her glasses, and picked up the glasses, but she never mailed the report. We were walking one day and she said something to the effect that she needed to mail in the report for the glasses assignment she had done last month. I made her aware of the due dates, and she was really disappointed. So make sure that you are aware of the due dates and that you get your reports in on time.

The Form

Filling out the form is the next most important task as a mystery shopper. This industry is dependent on your ability to fill out a form properly, and if the company has to contact you because information is missing, it may not be contacting you for additional assignments. Therefore, make sure that the entire form is complete. Review it twice if necessary.

The Scenario, Research, and Acquiring Knowledge

Whether you are visiting a grocery store or an apartment complex, you will be asked to complete certain scenarios or act out certain scenes in the play of life. Those of you who have had acting lessons or played in high school drama will love this part of the job. In one assignment I had to pretend that I wanted to purchase a three-carat diamond ring, and in another scenario I was asked to pose as a bride and try on wedding dresses. For the most part, you get to play pretend and acquire additional knowledge for free. For example, my husband and I were getting ready to purchase a new bed. Our current one was in the shape of a taco shell, and we were desperate. I placed a message on a board asking if anyone was aware of which companies shopped new mattress stores. I acquired a couple of company names and shopped almost all the new mattress stores in Arizona. By the end of the month, we had decided which mattress we wanted to purchase and where to purchase it. Because I used mystery shopping as a resource, we purchased a $3,000 mattress for $800, and I made approximately $300 doing the research I would have been doing anyway. You can use mystery shopping for new car research, new home construction, or any other purposes you choose. I have found excellent dining establishments that I currently frequent and spend my own money at, as well as hotels that I recommend to family and friends.

Submitting the Report

Please be aware of how the organization requires you to return the form or data. Some organizations require you to both phone in the report and mail in an original copy with the receipt. These assignments may be time-consuming, for you may be placed on hold or receive a recorded message, thus requiring you to continue to make contact in order to report the data. Next, the organization may want you to enter the data on a Microsoft Word form that is emailed to you as an attachment. You simply fill out the form, save it to your computer, and then send it via email as an attachment. In addition, snail mail is a common method for submitting reports; in such cases, the form typically has carbon copies, and the shopper retains the last copy for his or her records. Another method is to fill out the form online via the company's web site. This is a paperless process and typically results in a confirmation number after you submit your report online. However, if you have a dial-up Internet system, you may lose your data while you are entering a report if the system disconnects. Therefore, you may want to consider switching to a company that offers DSL access. Additionally, you will receive emails at a more rapid speed with DLS than with the dial-up system. Should your Internet system be nonfunctional, you will need a backup plan for entering your data. Local libraries often offer free access, and it would be wise to obtain a library card in case this issue should occur. Whatever the specified method of submission is, be aware of it and follow the proper procedures.

In this industry, no news is good news. After you submit the report, if possible ask for a confirmation number and the name of person you spoke to, and record the date and time you submitted the report. You will not receive praise or feedback on the assignment. Your recognition and reward is the offer of future assignments. If a company does not receive your assignment after you have submitted it, the company will be contacting you. You will not be contacted unless something is wrong or if the company wishes to give you future assignments. I did once receive a spontaneous $50 in the mail as a bonus for being a wonderful shopper, but this is very rare.

Conflicts and Independent Contractor Agreements

Many organizations utilize several different mystery-shopping agencies, so it is important to be aware of the types of conflicts that may occur. First, you are allowed to work for as many different agencies as you desire; however, you may not complete one assignment for two different agencies. For example, ABC Company asks you to visit the Randy's on Main Street for lunch tomorrow, and then you receive a call from DEF Company for the same location on the same day at the same time. If you accept both assignments, you are creating a conflict of interest and may be subject to a lawsuit. Simply tell DEF Company that you are busy and offer alternative dates. You may visit the same restaurant for two different companies, but not on the same day and at the same time.

Additionally, upon receiving your application and assignment information, you may receive a document called an independent contractor agreement. This document simply states legalities, such as the conflict of interest mentioned previously, as well as an agreement that you are aware of your individual responsibility to pay your own taxes. Next, it will state that you will be open to litigation if you open a mystery-shopping company within 2 years and utilize the company's forms or steal its customers. Finally, it will ask that you keep all information acquired at shopping locations confidential and private.

Here is a sample of an independent contractor agreement.

Terms and Conditions

In order for you to be a mystery shopper for The Great Mystery Shopping Company, LLC, you must accept all of the following terms and conditions:

This agreement is between you and The Great Mystery Shopping Company, LLC. Upon receiving this Independent Contractor Agreement and Application, you will be entered in our database as an Independent Contractor (IC); however, you will not have employee status. You may be called upon to perform, on a random basis, mystery shops/evaluations of scheduled assignments. Your responsibility will be to complete assignments according to instructions provided. Materials are distributed via email, fax, or U.S. Postal Service.

You promise to complete the assignment during the proper time and date perameters as well as return it in the proper manner as indicated in the instructions. The Great Mystery Shopping Company, LLC will not pay for work that is incomplete or submitted beyond the set due date. The IC will receive payment within sixty (60) days of submitting the assignment. The IC must additionally submit an invoice with the final report for payment by The Great Mystery Shopping Company, LLC.

Due to the fact that you are not classified as an employee, but rather as an independent contractor, The Great Mystery Shopping Company, LLC will not be deducting taxes from payments to you. Therefore, it is your sole responsibility to file and pay all federal, state, and local taxes. Additionally, you must adhere to all federal, state, and local tax laws as a self-employed individual. In accordance with federal tax law, The Great Mystery Shopping Company, LLC will mail to IC a completed tax form 1099, if IC's fee income (not expenses) exceeds $600 during a calendar year. The IC understands that he or she is not an employee and will not be covered under any type of worker's compensation insurance.

The Great Mystery Shopping Company, LLC is not liable for any malicious act undertaken by the IC and may revoke this contract at any given time.

The IC agrees to return any materials provided by The Great Mystery Shopping Company, LLC within 48 hours of the company's demanding said materials or within 48 hours of revoking the said contract. Additionally, the IC agrees to remain anonymous and professional at all times during assignments. The IC agrees that he or she will not take visible notes. The IC agrees not to open a mystery-shopping company for 2 years. The IC agrees not to share or utilize any confidential materials provided. The IC agrees that he or she will not share the outcome of the assessment with others. If an assignment requires two shoppers, the second shopper falls under the same confidentiality perameters, and the IC agrees to disclose all information to the second shopper. The IC is responsible for the behavior of the second shopper and agrees to said responsibility. Failure to adhere to these terms may result in litigation. If any litigation shall occur due to failure to comply by the IC, the IC agrees to pay all legal fees of The Great Mystery Shopping Company, LLC.

_____   _____
Independent Contractor   Great Mystery Shopping Co., LLC

When Are You an Independent Contractor?

The courts have considered many facts in deciding whether a worker is an independent contractor or an employee. The relevant facts fall into three main categories: behavioral control, financial control, and relationship of the parties. In each case, it is very important to consider all the facts—no single fact provides the answer. Carefully review the following IRS definitions.

Behavioral Control

These facts indicate whether the business has a right to direct or control how the worker does the work. A worker is an employee when the business has the right to direct and control that worker. The business does not have to actually direct or control the way the work is done, as long as it has the right to do so. For example:

- *Instructions.* If you receive extensive instructions on how work is to be done, this suggests that you are an employee. Instructions can cover a wide range of topics, such as how, when, or where to do the work and what tools or equipment to use.

- If you receive less extensive instructions about what should be done, and not about how it should be done, you may be an independent contractor. For instance, instructions about time and place may be less important than directions on how the work is performed.
- If the business provides you with training in required procedures and methods, this indicates that the business wants the work done in a certain way, and this suggests that you may be an employee.

Financial Control

These facts show whether you have a right to direct or control the business part of the work. For example:

- *Significant investment.* If you have a significant investment in your work, you may be an independent contractor. While there is no precise dollar test, the investment must have substance. However, a significant investment is not necessary to be an independent contractor.
- *Expenses.* If you are not reimbursed for some or all business expenses, then you may be an independent contractor, especially if your unreimbursed business expenses are high.
- *Opportunity for profit or loss.* If you can realize a profit or incur a loss, this suggests that you are in business for yourself and that you may be an independent contractor.

Relationship of the Parties

These are facts that illustrate how the business and the worker perceive their relationship. For example:

- *Employee benefits.* If you receive benefits, such as insurance, pension, or paid leave, this is an indication that you may be an employee. If you do not receive benefits, however, you could be either an employee or an independent contractor.
- *Written contracts.* A written contract may show what both you and the business intend. This may be very significant if it is difficult, if not impossible, to determine status based on other facts.

Which Are You?

For federal tax purposes, this is an important distinction. Your classification affects how you pay your federal income tax and your social security and Medicare taxes, and how you file your tax return. Your classification affects your eligibility for employee benefits and social security and Medicare benefits, and also affects your tax responsibilities. If you aren't sure of your work status, you should find out now.

When You Are an Employee

- Your employer must withhold income tax and your portion of social security and Medicare taxes. Also, your employer is responsible for paying social security, Medicare, and unemployment (FUTA) taxes on your wages. Your employer must give you a Form W-2, Wage and Tax Statement, showing the amount of taxes withheld from your pay.

- You may deduct employee business expenses for which you are not reimbursed on Schedule A of your income tax return, but only if you itemize deductions and these expenses total more than 2 percent of your adjusted gross income.

When You Are an Independent Contractor

- The business may be required to give you Form 1099-MISC, Miscellaneous Income, to report what it has paid to you.

- You are responsible for paying your own income tax and self-employment tax (Self-Employment Contributions Act, or SECA). The business does not withhold taxes from your pay. You may need to make estimated tax payments during the year to cover your tax liabilities.

- You may deduct business expenses on Schedule C of your income tax return.

IRS Tax Publications

If you are not sure whether you are an employee or an independent contractor, get Form SS-8, Determination of Employee Work Status for Purposes of Federal Employment Taxes and Income Tax Withholding. Publication 15-A, Employer's Supplemental Tax Guide, provides additional information on independent contractor status.

IRS Electronic Services

You may download and print IRS publications, forms, and other tax information materials on the Internet at www.irs.gov, and you may call the IRS at 1-800-829-3676 (1-800-TAX-FORM) to order free tax publications and forms. From a fax machine, dial (703) 368-9694 and you will immediately get a list of IRS tax forms faxed back to you. Follow the voice prompts to get specific forms faxed to you. Publication 1796, Federal Tax Products on CD-ROM, giving current and prior year tax publications and forms, can be purchased from the National Technical Information Service (NTIS). You may order Publication 1796 toll-free through the IRS at 1-877-233-6767 or via the Internet at www.irs.gov/cdorders.

Shopping with Small Children

Many shoppers are "stay-at-home moms" and shop with small children. This is perfectly fine if it is OK with the mystery-shopping company and the setting is appropriate. For example, a five-star restaurant would have couples celebrating an anniversary or business associates engaging in deals. Therefore, a screaming 9-month-old baby would be something out of the norm and might identify you as a shopper. However, establishments like family pizza places are comfortable for small children, and you are encouraged to bring them.

Another issue that I personally have had to face is when your child is having an off day. I was once in a grocery store and was trying to obtain all my interactions and associate names when my son, who was 2 at the time, started to throw a tantrum. A normal customer with a child would have said, forget it for today! The customer would have promptly left the store. However, I felt stuck, and I had an obligation to meet. So I toughed it out through the store and had a horrible experience, which consequently was reflected in my report. How was the bakery person supposed to respond to an angry mother with a screaming 2-year-old who was throwing cookies at her? I created a negative situation, and the response was appropriate for the situation, but how could I write someone up for not welcoming me to the bakery department when I could not hear her over my son's screaming?

So here is the recommendation: If you simply cannot calm down your little angel, go home, call the contracting company, and reschedule. The company will understand; in fact, it almost expects this. Be humble, and the company will work with you. Remember, this industry is made up almost entirely of stay-at-home moms and retired adults. Companies expect you to become sick, have doctor's appointments, and have bad days. Communicate your situation and your needs, and companies will be happy to work with you.

Rejecting an Assignment

On occasion you may have to turn down an assignment. Another commonly asked question is, "I turned down an assignment; will this hurt my chances of working for that company and receiving future assignments?" My answer is yes and no. There are several reasons why one might turn down an assignment. The example that I usually give is that of a bookstore assignment that I had to turn down. I was notified of a bookstore assignment, and as an instructor I accepted it immediately. I received the information in the mail a couple of days later, only to find out that it was an adult bookstore! Well, I did not want to even see what the store would demonstrate or have to suggestive sell. So I promptly called the company and stated that it was not a good match. In addition, I stated that if I were offered assignments in a different industry, I would be glad to establish a business relationship with the company in the future. I feel that in this situation, more information should have been exchanged, so it is important to ask questions about the assignment when you are originally offered it. I did not hear from this company again; however, I didn't really want to work for it anyway. This is a fact that you should remember as a shopper: *You have the choice to accept or reject an assignment at any time. It is the personal freedom that comes with being a business owner.*

Another situation would be that you are going on vacation and have to turn down an assignment. Humbly turn down the assignment by offering alternative dates for the visit or request an assignment for the following month. Regardless, ask the company to please keep you in its database and exhibit a strong desire to work with it in the near future.

Canceling an Assignment

A situation may arise in your personal life in which you will have to cancel a previously assigned shop. In this situation, communication is the key. I once became extremely ill and had to cancel a week's worth of assignments. Basically, I recommend calling the company and speaking with the person who originally assigned the shop to you. Explain to that person that you are having a personal or medical problem and are unable to complete the assignment. You may want to offer future dates or names of friends who may be interested in completing the assignment. If you are unable to speak to someone, leave a voice message or send an urgent email. Doing nothing will not create a positive business relationship, so once again communication is the key.

Another industry no-no is having someone else complete the shop for you. This person may not be aware of the details of the shop, and it is your reputation that is on the line. Additionally, most independent contractor agreements state that you will not subcontract out any of your assignments. If it is revealed that someone other than you, the contracting agent, completed the assignment, you may be subjecting yourself to a lawsuit. So beware of the rules and restrictions before you act.

Assignment Distribution

Assignment distribution is a random factor depending solely on the company offering the assignments. Some locations are shopped three times a day, with shoppers rotated on a daily basis. Others are shopped quarterly, with shoppers rotated every quarter. Depending on the situation, you could receive an assignment the day before, a month in advance, or three months in advance. The typical scheduler will contact you 2 to 3 weeks in advance and ask if you would like an assignment for the following month. Therefore, when you begin making contacts, you will probably receive your first assignment approximately 1 month later because the current month's assignments have already been scheduled.

Additionally, you may want to keep track of the method and frequency of assignment distribution by each company. For example, ABC mystery-shopping company may send out a card every month with a date for you to call in for assignments depending on the first letter of your last name. Also, several companies may post their assignments on the Internet on a certain date and at a certain time. They then send an email to their shopper base stating that the assignments have been posted. If you are aware of when a company posts its assignments, you can visit the site before the posting has been publicly announced and therefore have your choice of all assignments. I frequently mark my calendar for these particular days and also use a calendar on my Microsoft email program. This program alerts me of certain dates and times when I should make contacts and is a continuous as well as a recurring list. However, a spreadsheet with the company name, contact information, method of contact, passwords or usernames, and frequency of assigning shops should be sufficient. Remember, the early bird gets the worm, and persistence is the key to becoming successful in this industry.

Finally, most assignments are scheduled for the beginning of the month. Should something occur, there is a cushion for completion at the end of the month. Therefore, you will be completing most assignments in the first and last weeks of the month, with the middle of the month being an industry dry spell.

Rating and Testing

Many companies may ask you to take a competency test before you are assigned a location. Basically, you will read the instructions, review the forms, and take a brief test of the knowledge you acquired to prove that you comprehended the parameters of the assignment. Additionally, once you have completed an assignment, the assignment may be rated on quality with stars or levels. For example, you may complete an apartment assignment and do an excellent job that earns the maximum of four stars. Ultimately, when the scheduling agency is distributing assignments for the following month, it will contact all the four-star contractors/shoppers first. Finally, a few companies will ask you to take a test every 6 months to will determine what level or rank of shopper you are and thus will provide you with a raise per hour or per assignment.

CHAPTER

7

The Shop

Each company will ask for different components to be analyzed; however, there are several common factors. These factors are cleanliness, customer service, quality control, hazards, and organization and stocking.

Cleanliness

Cleanliness can consist of such things as freshly vacuumed floors, clean windows, clean walls, and proper maintenance of the restroom. Some companies may ask you to go to extreme measures in evaluating cleanliness, such as looking under the bed in a hotel room or performing the "white glove test" on various wall hangings.

Customer Service

It is very important not to allow the service provided by the associate to manipulate the outcome of the report. For example, if the associate is absolutely wonderful, but she is not wearing a visible name tag, you must deduct the point for not wearing a name tag. In cases where the employee is extremely negative, try to take a deep breath and remain neutral to evaluate him or her as a professional. The information must not be tainted because your experience was wonderful or bad. Even if the associate was cruel, do not look for areas where you can mark him or her down.

Remember, the main reason you are being paid to visit the location is to catch the employee doing the right thing. If for some reason he or she is not giving 100 percent, you can help him or her to improve by being honest with your evaluations. Additionally, if you are not being treated with the utmost respect, simply remind yourself that the corporate leaders of the organization are paying you and that your word is golden. They are listening because they are paying you for information. Rest assured that if you record the employee's actions in a factual manner, the employee will perhaps receive either critical reviews or raises based on your opinion. So consider it as a service to the community that promotes mutual respect for all with high-quality service and products offered.

Next, you may be asked the exact phrase with which you were greeted, or what was said in terms of suggestive selling. For example, "Welcome to McDonald's; how may I help you?" or, "Would you like fries with that?" In any case, be sure you note any exact wording that must be identified before you begin the shop.

Finally, almost 99 percent of the time you will be asked to provide the name of the employee, and 50 percent of the time you will need to provide a description of the employee—age, race, sex, hair color, height, weight, and sometimes even eye color.

Quality Control

Quality control can involve a number of elements, from food freshness to the number of asparagus tips on your plate. Fast food restaurants have issues with this component. French fries alone can be hard, cold, oversalted, soggy, or burned. It can also relate to issues such as if your steak prepared as desired.

Hazards

I consider this component to be by far one of the most important components. You will be asked to note various problems that might harm the customers, vendors, or employees. Several companies do not include this component as part of their reports, which I believe to be very unfortunate. In fact, my comments on hazards have been rejected quite often when this is not a component of the report. Nonetheless, you will often be asked to report conditions such as ripped carpet, unlocked doors in hotels after hours, moldy food in play areas (ball pits), or an associate providing a room key to a guest without proper identification.

I recall one time when I was completing a hotel shop. I heard noises in the hall that woke my son and me up very early. We were bored, so I finished most of my report and packed up. Now picture this: I had my bag on one arm, my laptop on the other, my son's Scooby Doo backpack on my back, his little bag in one hand, and his little hand in the other. It was the Christmas season, and the hotel was very crowded. The hotel staff had decided that Christmas week would be the perfect week to remodel! When we stepped out of our room and into the corridor, we saw that the carpet was rolled up diagonally from the ceiling to the floor and that the baseboards had been removed, exposing 3-inch nails! In addition, there were workers on their knees with power tools everywhere. I had to maneuver around all the obstacles like an Indiana Jones adventure! I finally made it to the front desk and was greeted with a warm and friendly hello. The associate asked how my stay was, and I mentioned the work in the hall. She simply smiled and handed me a white sheet of paper with "Excuse Our Mess" written on it. She then stated, "Didn't you receive this?" I said no, and said that if I had been aware of these hazards, I would have requested another level or location in the hotel. The associate did nothing to remedy the situation, and I included all this information in my report as being both hazardous and unprofessional.

Organization and Stocking

This area may consist of anything from the stocking and organization of clothing to the stocking of bathroom supplies or condiments on a table. Assignments will vary, but it is important that you are aware of exactly what the company is looking for.

Pan the store with your eyes and note whether it is pleasant to the eye and organized appropriately. Note whether shelves are nicely stocked and whether racks of clothing offer a variety of sizes and colors. A good example of proper organization and stocking is The Gap. Everything is nicely folded, and if your size is not visible, the associate is on a headset to others in the stockroom who will retrieve your size immediately. Examples of poorly stocked and organized stores are Marshall's, TJ Maxx, and Ross. Many times as a regular customer I have observed racks jammed with clothing and severely missized. In addition, other racks have one piece of clothing hanging by itself and falling off a hanger.

Tools and Tricks

As a beginner, you may often wonder, how am I going to memorize all this information for the report? Eventually you will establish your own style and method for acquiring names of sales associates and such. However, I have listed several tips below to help get you started:

- If an employee is not wearing a name tag, simply ask the employee's name or say that he or she looks familiar and offer your name first.
- Bring a hand-size note pad and take notes in the dressing room or restroom.
- Bring a small tape recorder and record in the dressing room, in the restroom, or into your purse.
- Call yourself on your cell phone and leave a message.
- Scan the room for cleanliness, and if you don't see anything obvious, then it is most likely fine.
- Bring your first assignments with you and leave them under the seat of your car. If you forgot a component of the report, you can return right away and obtain the information.

Note Taking

Another skill is note taking and abbreviations. I recommend that you utilize a three-by-five-inch index card and list the information required for the assignment. For example, if you are shopping a grocery store, you should list each area of review on the card, such as:

Butcher

Baker

Deli

Cashier

Employee 1

Employee 2

Also include other pertinent data, such as "visit the restroom" or "record number of open and closed checkout stations."

Next, you must learn a system of abbreviations, such as WFBL for for white female blonde.

The final results of the visit would be something like this:

Butcher: Carl, W, M, bald, 40s, 6—Nice and helpful

Baker: Cindy, Hisp, F, Bl, 30s, 5'7"—Very busy, mentioned specials

Deli: Jane, Hisp, F, Br, 30s, 5'2"—Provided recipes

Cashier: Brenda, W, F, 20s, 5'5"—Chatted with the bagger the entire time

Employee 1: Glen, W, M, Br, 20s, 6'—Stocking the freezer, answered all my questions

Employee 2 : Sally, W, F, Br, 20s, 5'2"—Stocking the health and beauty area—nice smile

R/R: Very dirty and in need of stocking

Stations: 4 open, 8 closed—total of 12

Commonly Used Abbreviations

Sex

M	Male
F	Female

Race

Hisp	Hispanic
A	Asian
W	Caucasian
AA	African American
Nat	Native American
PI	Pacific Islander

Body Image

H	Heavy-set
M	Medium
S	Small

Other

R/R Restroom

Recording Devices

You will need a watch with a second hand to complete many assignments. Several companies instruct the shopper to assess the time period during which an action occurs or between two actions. They want the exact measurement of time in minutes and seconds. For example:

- The period from time you enter the line until the time you ordered
- The time period between placing an order and receiving your food
- The time from your entering the facility until you are greeted
- The time lapse between food courses
- The time period before following up for satisfaction
- The time period between submitting payment and receiving the processed transaction

Many shoppers purchase microrecorders as a way of tracking notes. Also, a company may require that you record a specific interaction or conversation. Finally, many companies are requesting that you purchase a digital camera to record images of the employees and atmosphere. These devices are not mandatory or required to become a mystery shopper, however, if you are seeking higher-end assignments, you may want to eventually invest in them.

How Shoppers Get Caught

There are many ways in which one can be uncovered as a shopper.

- Being so nervous that it is blatantly obvious that you are a shopper.
- Taking notes in plain view.
- Staring at the associate's name tag.
- Stating that you are a mystery shopper and the associate had better treat you right or you will write him or her up! Remember, you are to be anonymous at all times.
- Rushing. Many new shoppers or full-time shoppers schedule too many shops in one day. They make the mistake of running into a store, buying anything with the right purchase price, and then running out. This is a dead giveaway.

- Visiting the same location too many times, to the point of recognition. For example, you can visit a cell phone store only so many times within a month before the employees figure out that you are a shopper.

Why Shoppers Do Not Get
Additional Assignments

The obvious reasons why shoppers do not get contacted for additional assignments are either that they got caught or that they did not adhere to the constraints of the assignment. Perhaps the shopper visited the wrong location or went on the wrong day or at the wrong time. However, if you are too nervous or obtuse, it will be obvious that you are shopping. Not too many customers get nervous asking about meat in a grocery store, nor do they question the knowledge of the butcher. Another big clincher is the fact that many shoppers do not get a receipt. Your receipt is proof that you visited the location and is a major component of the assignment. One unethical practice is called "tabletop shopping." This practice involves calling a location and getting a name for the form without actually visiting the a establishment, then falsifying data on a report. The practice of tabletop shopping is a form of career suicide. Another unethical practice is to take an old report and submit it as a new experience for a different engagement. In other words, you were assigned three locations, and you submitted the same data or portions thereof for all three. The final way to commit career suicide is to use curse words or to describe others and events in an unprofessional manner with opinionated language.

Spice Up Those Reports

When writing assignments, these words or terms may be used:

Positive
Attractive, organized, fair, lovely, pretty, beautiful, clean, immaculate, spotless, bright, sparkling, fresh, airy, well organized, appealing, welcoming, inviting, enticing, enchanting, fascinating, tidy, artistic, orderly, shipshape, spic-and-span, appealing

Negative
Distasteful, repelling, dingy, grimy, grubby, filthy, dirty, messy, unkempt, disorganized, muddled, cluttered, smelly, dusty, sordid, foul, cramped, disarray, musty

When describing customer service, use these terms:

Positive
Friendly, likable, professional, attentive, informative, knowledgeable, trustworthy, exceptional, polite, courteous, entertaining, considerate, skillful, enthusiastic, bubbly, eager, happy, jovial, pleasure, pleasing, communicative, expertly, well-groomed, charming, interesting, exuberant, exciting, delightful, confident, comfortable, relaxed, honest, respectful, composed, anxious, graceful, thoughtful, personable, agreeable, appreciative, loyal, fascinating, neighborly

Negative
Unfriendly, rude, disrespectful, preoccupied, unconcerned, nasty, hurried, confused, intrusive, indifferent, distracted, uncaring, ignorant, lacking, crude, dishonest, thoughtless, withdrawn, aloof, casual, remote, detached, nonchalant, hasty, hotheaded, angry, upset, illadvised, selfish, discourteous, routine, rehearsed, monotone, mumbled, too soft-spoken, bored, tired

Positive Phrases to Use

She treated me like an old friend.

I was appreciated as a customer.

I felt I was valued as a customer because. . . .

Welcomed me into . . . .

Greeted me by saying. . . .

Thanked me by saying…

Quickly assessed my needs.

Asked detailed qualifying questions.

Expertly explained.

Friendly bond.

Interacted well with customers.

Successfully made my visit a memorable one.

Tailored the presentation to my needs.

I would definitely recommend the business.

Made me feel comfortable by. . . .

Made me feel my needs were important.

Listened attentively to me.

Sold me on the services.

They encouraged me to. . . .

I will surely return because. . . .

The atmosphere was. . . .

The general mood was. . . .

They seemed genuinely interested in helping me.

A very professional and considerate employee.

Welcomed me like an appreciated guest.

Engaged in conversation with me.

Initiated the sale.

Tried to upscale or suggestive sell merchandise.

Gave me adequate information.

Asked me to return.

Gave me their full attention.

Refrained from nonbusiness matters.

Knowledgeable about the products/service.

Went out of their way to. . . .

Approached customers in a courteous manner.

Sincerely thanked me.

Gave a wonderful sales presentation.

Explained features, benefits, and warrantees skillfully.

Negative Phrases to Use

It seemed as if they wanted to be elsewhere.

They couldn't have cared less.

I felt I was disturbing them.

I felt I was imposing, rushed, not important.

I felt ignored because. . . .

I would not give them my business because. . . .

Additional report-writing resources can be found at http://www.mysteryshopisland.com/writingtools.html.

The Do's and Don'ts of Mystery Shopping

Do's

Give the associate the opportunity to suggestive sell and demonstrate items.

Be fair and objective.

Get names and descriptions.

Set up a scenario before you enter the location, and allow the associate to fulfill all the categories.

Write in complete sentences, using proper grammar and spelling.

Ask questions and continue to learn.

Meet the time constraints of the assignment

Communicate a need for an extension of the assignment.

Catch the employee doing the right thing and praise her or him.

Check for congruency in all areas of the report.

Don'ts

Forget to get names.

Be afraid of entering a store.

Rush.

Delay processing paperwork.

Submit a report in an incorrect manner.

Utilize opinions.

Forget to communicate a need for an extension.

Skim through instructions.

Announce that you are a shopper.

Get caught taking notes.

Stare at name tags.

Business Law

Please make sure that you keep up with the laws regarding secret shopping in your city and state. To discover the current laws in your state, go to your local county web site. It should have a section that will allow you to review an up-to-date listing of current regulations. After you find the state regulations, review all information on private investigators or secret shoppers.

Here are several links that may help.

State and Law Research

Law Research	www.lawresearch.com
State Legislatures	www.ncsl.org
State Links	www.50states.com
County Links	www.naco.org
Licensing	http://www.crimetime.com/licensing.htm

State Laws

It is *illegal* to mystery-shop in the state of *Nevada* without a private investigator's license. To my dismay, what appears to be occurring is that mystery-shopping organizations or market research agencies are utilizing shoppers in the traditional way. If they are caught and indicted, they simply reveal the names of the shoppers. The mystery-shopping companies are released from all charges, and the shoppers are penalized. Another method is when companies hire you as an employee working under a P.I. and thus withhold taxes. Therefore, you cannot write off any of your expenses as business expenses, for you are an employee, not a contracting agent.

In the state of *Florida*, the only legal mystery shops are customer service shops of restaurants. Therefore, if you take part in an integrity restaurant assignment or an assignment in any other type of industry, you are breaking the law and may be subject to a fine or penalty.

All secret shoppers should be knowledgeable about Nevada and Florida laws:

Nevada laws and statutes (search private investigator—type of work), www.leg.state.nv.us/nrs/nrs%2D648.html

Florida laws and statutes (search private investigator—type of work), www.flsenate.gov

General Business Questions

This site http://3mom.com/html/business_law.html answers such general business questions as

Can I run a business out of my home?

What is a business?

Do I need insurance?

Do I need any licenses or permits?

Do I need a taxpayer identification number?

What do I need to start a business?

Do I need a fictitious business name statement?

A bond was required for my occupational licensing. Why do I need one?

All secret shoppers should be familiar with applicable private investigative laws in their state. These can be found at the following sites:

Alabama   http://www.legislature.state.al.us/

Alaska   http://w3.legis.state.ak.us/home.html

Arizona	http://www.azleg.state.az.us/
Arkansas	http://www.arkleg.state.ar.us/
California	http://www.leginfo.ca.gov/
Colorado	http://www.state.co.us/gov_dir/stateleg.html
Connecticut	http://www.cga.state.ct.us/
Delaware	http://www.legis.state.de.us/Legislature.nsf/?Opendatabase
District of Columbia	http://www.dccouncil.washington.dc.us/
Florida	http://www.leg.state.fl.us/
Georgia	http://www2.state.ga.us/legis/
Hawaii	http://www.capitol.hawaii.gov/
Idaho	http://www2.state.id.us/legislat/legislat.html
Illinois	http://www.legis.state.il.us/
Indiana	http://www.ai.org/legislative/
Iowa	http://www.legis.state.ia.us/
Kansas	http://www.kslegislature.org/
Kentucky	http://www.lrc.state.ky.us/index.htm
Louisiana	http://www.legis.state.la.us/
Maine	http://janus.state.me.us/legis/
Maryland	http://mlis.state.md.us/
Massachusetts	http://www.state.ma.us/legis/
Michigan	http://www.michiganlegislature.org/
Minnesota	http://www.leg.state.mn.us/
Mississippi	http://www.ls.state.ms.us/
Missouri	http://www.moga.state.mo.us/
Montana	http://leg.state.mt.us/css/default.asp
Nebraska	http://www.unicam.state.ne.us/index.htm
Nevada	http://www.leg.state.nv.us/
New Hampshire	http://gencourt.state.nh.us/ie/
New Jersey	http://www.njleg.state.nj.us/

New Mexico	http://legis.state.nm.us/
New York	http://www.nysl.nysed.gov/ils/legislature/ legis.html
North Carolina	http://www.ncga.state.nc.us/homePage.pl
North Dakota	http://www.state.nd.us/lr/
Ohio	http://www.legislature.state.oh.us/search.cfm
Oklahoma	http://www.lsb.state.ok.us/
Oregon	http://www.leg.state.or.us/
Pennsylvania	http://www.legis.state.pa.us/
Rhode Island	http://www.rilin.state.ri.us/
South Carolina	http://www.scstatehouse.net/
South Dakota	http://legis.state.sd.us/index.cfm
Tennessee	http://www.legislature.state.tn.us/sitemap.htm
Texas	http://www.capitol.state.tx.us/
Utah	http://www.le.state.ut.us/
Vermont	http://www.leg.state.vt.us/
Virginia	http://legis.state.va.us/
Washington	http://www.leg.wa.gov/wsladm/default.htm
West Virginia	http://www.legis.state.wv.us/
Wisconsin	http://www.legis.state.wi.us/
Wyoming	http://legisweb.state.wy.us/

Current Litigation and Legislation

Contract Worker Law

A new law has been enacted aimed at discovering independent contract workers who have been avoiding paying child support. In light of this, you may be asked to provide your current information monthly in order to adhere to this new law.

Go to the following link to find the legislation for your review:

https://newhirereporting.com/OH-Newhire/FAQ.asp?State=OH

New hire reporting is a valuable tool that contributes to the well-being of many families and assists in preventing fraudulent unemployment payments and/or welfare benefit payments. If you have received a notice from the state that referred to a lack of compliance, or if you have additional questions about complying with the new hire reporting law, please contact your local state government or www.irs.gov.

Multistate Legislation

The following material is a submission from MSPA:

Mystery Shopping Providers Association Update

There are three states, Arizona, Nevada, and Illinois where Mystery Shopping Providers Association (MSPA) is currently seeking amendments to the Private Investigator Laws in order to allow mystery shoppers to operate without a Private Investigator (P.I.) license. The MSPA supports the need for a license when "integrity-based" shops are done if an employee could be prosecuted or terminated.

The focus of the MSPA is to make sure companies and shoppers:

(I) Are trained and certified by the Mystery Shopping Providers Association or its successor organization;

(II) Enter into an agreement with the Mystery Shopping Providers Association or its successor organization requiring the person to comply with the professional standards and ethics of the Mystery Shopping Providers Association or the successor organization; and

(III) Are provided to the business, business organization, or governmental entity by a business that is a member of the Mystery Shopping Providers Association or its successor organization, if the business enters into an agreement with the Mystery Shopping Providers Association or its successor organization requiring the business to comply with the professional standards and ethics of the Mystery Shopping Providers Association or the successor organization.

  I. A person is not required to comply with the provisions of subparagraph (5) of paragraph (m) of subsection I if:

    (a) The Mystery Shopping Providers Association or its successor organization ceases to exist; and

(b) At the time the person acts as a customer or client of the business, business organization or governmental entity, no organization exists that performs functions similar to the functions performed by the Mystery Shopping Providers Association or its successor organization.

Business Ethics

As a private contractor in the market research business, it is important that you conduct your business with the highest degree of integrity and ethics. To start, review all applicable laws and statutes regarding independent contract status. After all applicable laws and statutes have been reviewed, the next major step for independent contractors is entering into a short- or long-term contract (see the discussion of contracts in Chapter 7) with a mystery-shopping company. A private contractor is required to thoroughly review all independent contract or agreements and acquire a clear understanding of the terms *confidentiality* and *anonymity*. When assignments become available and a contractor meets the criteria, mystery-shopping companies may contact the contractor via email, telephone, fax, or U.S. mail. Before accepting any assignments, a contractor must acknowledge any possible conflicts of interest (e.g., family or friends on the staff, preconceived opinions about the assignment, and so on). If there is a conflict of interest, the contractor should decline the assignment. The contractor should contact the mystery-shopping company immediately when conflicts of interest are possible.

When it is determined that a conflict of interest does not exist, then a contractor should accept and complete the assignment. A contractor should complete the assignment according to the instructions that have been provided by the mystery-shopping company.

In order to avoid being labeled as a shopper, a contractor should rotate assignments.

Do not enter this industry if you are unable to accurately record factual details.

Do not enter this industry if you are in the habit of applying minimal effort.

As discussed in Chapter 7, tabletop shopping is unethical. It is the act of calling a location, getting a name for the form without visiting the actual establishment, and then falsifying data on a report. The practice of tabletop shopping is the first in committing career suicide.

The Number of Mystery Shops

Many mystery-shopping programs assume one visit per outlet. However, it is generally believed that multiple assessments allow a fairer and more objective appraisal than a single assessment. This provides a much more complete picture of what is happening, enabling an averaging out of performance rather than one judgment. Therefore, the responsiblility of assignment rotation should rest on the shopper as well as the contracting organization. Several assessments from one individual contractor could result in skewed or misleading data. For the integrity of the industry as well as to remain anonymous, a shopper must effectively rotate visits to individual locations.

The general recommendation for each location given by industry standards is to make at least two personal visits and two telephone contacts to the same outlet every other month, while at the same time acknowledging the client's individual requirements. In other words, do not shop an individual location to the point of recognition even if you have the opportunity to do so.

Schedulers

A scheduler is a private agency that receives funding from a mystery-shopping company to match shoppers to assignments. It has come to my attention that several scheduling organizations are demanding additional fees from shoppers in order to receive preferential treatment. This is not a standard or ethical business practice. Never pay a scheduler for an assignment or for preferential treatment.

Anonymity

Concealing the identity of a mystery-shopper can sometimes be a problem, particularly in rural or small-town outlets. To overcome this, scenarios should be simple and relevant to all outlets within the organization, regardless of location, and should not demand too much of the assessor in terms of acting as an ordinary customer. Additionally, the shopper should never announce his or her presence as an evaluator or take notes in the open.

Another ethical dilemma is related to who the shopper can share the activity and the career details with. A frequently asked question in my course is, "Can I tell my friends or my husband about my assignments?" The general ethical consensus is to reveal as little as possible. For example, if a shopper were to acquire food poisoning in a restaurant, can the shopper share this information and warn friends and family? The answer is no! You can state that you had a restaurant assignment, but you cannot reveal the location, the name of the establishment, or any of the details.

One exception to this rule is if you have an assignment that requires two shoppers. Then you may share the details of the assignment with the second shopper and record data from that shopper by referring to the person as shopper number two. Additionally, shopper number two may support your efforts by assisting with acquiring names and other helpful information. However, shopper number two must adhere to the same confidentiality agreement and anonymity as you, the shopper.

Most organizations provide the shopper with an identification number to be utilized in lieu of the shopper's name. This allows the individual locations to review the data that have been assessed. It is important that you not record data that would obviously link you as a shopper to the report. For example, you may want to record that you engaged in personal conversation rather than record the actual specifics of the conversation. The exceptions to this rule are auto and apartment assignments. To ensure the safety of the selling agent, you will be required to submit an ID before a test drive of a car or a tour of an apartment complex. Some apartment assessments require the selling agent to send a thank-you card or engage in a follow-up phone call. You will need to report the follow-up information to the mystery-shopping company as well.

Quality Control

Once the mystery-shopping assessment is complete, it is essential to check your questionnaires for validity, accuracy, consistency, and objectivity. Thus the data that a shopper records in the questionnaire must be consistent and congruent with the narrative and rating scales. For example, if a shopper rates the service as poor and later records positive service in the narrative portion, the report is incongruent and useless.

Objectivity

Objectivity can be defined as the use of factual information rather than opinions. A fact is verifiable and is usually verified by using numbers, dates, or policies and procedures. A fact is beyond argument if measuring devices and records are correct.

An opinion is a judgment. An opinion is changeable depending on who is interpreting the evidence or how the evidence is interpreted.

For example, identify each sentence below as a fact or an opinion.

Dorothy's work was poorly written.

Fact / Opinion

The statement is an opinion, for the word *poorly* is subjective.

Dorothy submitted all paperwork before the deadline.

Fact / Opinion

The statement is a fact because it can be verified by dates.

Links, Etiquette, and Ethics

The following section is a helpful source of useful links which will narrow your search for proper etiquette and ethics.

Business Links for Independent Contractors

http://www.mybizoffice.com

http://www.entrepreneur.com

http://www.startupbiz.com

http://www.inc.com

http://www.abusinessresource.com

http://www.businessknowhow.net

Organizations
http://www.nase.org

Business Etiquette
http://www.hbcollege.com/management/students/bus_etiquette.htm

---

MSPA Code of Professional Standards and Ethics Agreement for Mystery Shoppers

The Mystery Shopping Providers Association (MSPA) is dedicated to improving service and promoting excellence in the mystery shopping industry. A fundamental aim of the Association is to ensure that the highest standards and ethics are maintained. To improve the value and reputation and to stimulate the use of mystery shopping services, it is important that information about mystery shopping services is accurately communicated to both the business community and the public at large, while complying with applicable government laws, regulations and ordinances.

MSPA expects members and shoppers to follow principles of honesty, professionalism, fairness and confidentiality to guard the interests of the public and our clients in order to promote good business practices.

The Mystery Shopping Providers Association's Shopper's Code of Professional Standards is established to ensure that all MSPA certified shoppers conform to the following principles:

- Commit, in principle, to the purposes of the association: improving service and promoting excellence in the mystery shopping industry;

- Conduct mystery shopping services in an honest and ethical manner;

- Conduct mystery shopping services according to industry procedures and regulations set forth and agreed to by MSPA members;

- Instill confidence in mystery shopping and encourage public cooperation;

• Respect our MSPA members, clients and the general public.

In addition, we agree to the following Rules of Ethical Conduct:

- • I agree to perform all shops to the best of my ability;

- • I agree to perform all shops with honesty and integrity;

- • I agree to submit all reports on or before the deadline;

- • I agree to honor all confidentiality agreements;

- • I agree to give immediate notice to the shopping company if I cannot perform a shop for any reason;

- • I agree to return follow-up calls or emails in a timely manner;

- • I agree to keep paperwork and notes for at least 60 days in case questions arise by the client;

- • I will not perform a shop unless I have thoroughly read each question on the survey and the guidelines provided by the shopping provider;

- • I will not falsify or misrepresent reports;

- • I will not ask or encourage anyone to break confidentiality agreements with other firms for whom they conduct mystery shopping assignments;

- • I will not use any MSPA media to publish complaints against vendors, clients, shoppers or mystery shopper providers;

- • I will not share information with others on which company shops which clients;

- • I will not share information with others on shopping fees and reimbursements for specific clients;

- • I will not share the results of a shop with others in order to protect the client's confidentiality;

- • I will not perform any shops under the influence of illegal drugs or prescription drugs that might impair my abilities;

- • I agree not to become inebriated or drink beyond the legal limits set forth in my state or perform any other activity that my cause harm to myself or others while mystery shopping;

- I will not contact a client directly without approval of the shopping company;

- I will not disrupt the normal business flow of an operation in the process of performing a shop (do not cause a scene);

- I will not announce myself as a mystery shopper to the business being shopped unless given specific instructions by the shopping company;

- I will not accept a mystery shopping assignment for a business that I, my family or friends work for;

- I will not list any shopping company I work for as an "employer" on any forms (especially unemployment forms) if I am hired strictly as an independent contractor for that company.

The following is an insertion from Mike Green, current president of the MSPA:

Mystery Shopping Providers Association

The Mystery Shopping Providers Association was formed in 1998 to unite companies for the purpose of strengthening the mystery shopping industry through combined efforts and actions. It is the goal of the membership to improve and stimulate the acceptance, performance, reputation and use of mystery shopping services.

The MSPA is the largest professional trade association dedicated to improving service quality using anonymous resources. There is a North American chapter and a European chapter with more to come. Combined, there are member companies representing 20 countries around the world. Our diverse membership includes marketing research and merchandising companies, private investigation firms, training organizations and companies that specialize in providing mystery shopping services.

The primary goals of the MSPA are to:

1. Establish professional standards and ethics for the industry.

2. Educate providers, clients and shoppers to improve quality of service.

3. Improve the image of the industry through public relations and conduct.

4. Promote the membership to other industry associations and prospective clients.

Ethics: Each member company is required to sign an ethics and standards agreement before they are allowed to join MSPA. Our goal is to raise the bar for ethics and standards for the entire industry. Our members are held accountable for their actions where non-members are not.

Education: MSPA provides an annual convention and an annual workshop each year for the members. Through seminars and outside speakers, we continue to offer educational opportunities to keep our members informed and up to date on issues affecting our industry.

In 2003, due to popular request, the MSPA also started offering educational opportunities for shoppers around the country, both on-line and in full-day workshops. By completing the MSPA on-line course and the workshop, shoppers receive certification from the MSPA. Our members recognize this certification and many use the certification as one tool to aid in selecting the best shoppers to schedule. Other scheduling factors, of course, include experience, education, location, etc. When two shoppers are equally qualified, the MSPA certification is usually the tiebreaker.

Public Relations: The MSPA continues to provide announcements, information to national trade magazines on our activities. The MSPA office regularly handles requests for information and provides quotes to the media on customer service issues.

Promotions: The MSPA web page is the greatest marketing tool we have to advertise the mystery shopping industry, averaging 6 million hits a month. Our Marketing committee also advertises the MSPA in trade publications, on web pages and in other media outlets. The MSPA strives to bring attention to the industry so it will continue to grow in popularity.

Although governmental relations is not listed as a primary goal, the MSPA has been successful in changing outdated laws in California, Texas, Arizona and North Dakota which had negatively affected the mystery shopping and customer service industries. The MSPA is the watchdog for the industry.

Customer service has become a key factor in differentiation among companies. With profit margins slim, organizations are realizing that customer service remains the one area that can set them apart from their competitors. As the need for exceptional customer service increases, so does the need for mystery shopping services. The MSPA and its growing number of members worldwide see themselves as a key component in helping companies reach their goals for the future.

The Small Business and Payment

Stay Organized

In order to stay organized, you will need tracking forms and spreadsheets. I have found Michelle's web site to be extremely helpful and loaded with free organizational tools. The site is http://members.cox.net/m_herren/. It has the following forms:

Mystery Shopper Job Log

Mystery Shopper Company List

IRS Deduction Tracking Sheet

Credit Card Expense Sheet

Mystery Shopper Job Document

Mystery Shopper Company List Document

IRS Deductions Document

Other Forms

Daily Checklists   http://www.volition.com/mystery.html

Assignment logs   http://www.volition.com/mysteryother.html

MapQuest   www.mapquest.com

Gator Form Assistant   www.gator.com

Free Email and Fax

Just Shop Email	justshop.mail.everyone.net
Yahoo Mail	mail.yahoo.com
Hotmail	www.hotmail.com
Fax 4 Free	www.fax4free.com
EFax	www.efax.com

Commonly Utilized Forms

The following are commonly utilized forms that will assist you in organizing your mystery-shopping data. They are provided by the NCPMS, and I hope you find them helpful.

Termination of a Contract

Today's Date

Company Name Goes Here
Attn. Whoever Goes Here
Company Address Goes Here
Company City, State, Zip Goes Here

Dear _____,

I must formally cancel our independent contractor's agreement and contract. The cancellation will go into effect within 15 business days.

It has been a pleasure working with you and your company. I would like to personally thank you for the unique and wonderful opportunities that I experienced.

If you have any questions, please feel free to contact me at the address and phone number below.

Wishing you luck and success,

Your Name Goes Here
Your Email Address Goes Here
Your Contact Number Goes Here
Your Home Address Goes Here

* * * *

Sample Invoice

Niccole Rogers
P.O. Box 311573
Tampa, FL 33680
Tel. (813) 000-0000
Fax. (813) 000-0000
niccole@ncpmscenter.org

April 1, 2003

Great Mystery Shopping Co.
Attention: Billing
33 Anywhere Road
Anywhere, FL 33333

General Invoice for Services Rendered
March 1—March 31, 2003

March 1—Debby's Delicious Diner @ Fowler Ave..........$15.00 Flat Fee
March 3—Debby's Delicious Diner @ Bearss Ave..........$15.00 Flat Fee
March 26—Debby's Delicious Diner @ 26th St............$15.00 Flat Fee

Total Due: $45.00

Quick Payment/Contract Reference:
Paragraph 7, Line 2 of Contractor's Agreement states, "I fully under-stand that payment is issued on the 1st day of the month following my completed assignment."

Notification is requested if payment will not be issued or if payment will be issued on the agreed contract payment date.

* * * *

Confirming a Telephone Conversation

Today's Date

Company Name Goes Here
The Person You Spoke With Goes Here

Dear (the name of the person you spoke with goes here):

It was a pleasure speaking with you today, and I look forward to completing my new assignment.

During our telephone conversation, you indicated that the assignment should (type instructions and deadlines here).

Thank you for giving me this opportunity. I will be sure to contact you with any additional questions. ;-)

Sincerely,

Your Name Goes Here
Your Contact Information Goes Here

✳ ✳ ✳ ✳

Overdue Invoice

Niccole Rogers
P.O. Box 311573
Tampa, FL 33680
Tel. (813) 000-0000
Fax. (813) 000-0000
niccole@ncpmscenter.org

April 1, 2003
Great Merchandising Co.

Attention: Wanda Will
33 Anywhere Road
Anywhere, FL 33333
www.justshop.org
wanda@justshop.org

Re: Payment Overdue

Dear Ms. Will:

As of March 28, 2003, I have not received payment for services rendered in January 2003. All services were rendered as per your firm's instructions, and my invoice correctly reflects the amount of $75.00 due. Please issue payment for the overdue balance of $75.00 within the next 5 business days. If payment will not be issued within the next 5 business days, please call or email me so arrangements can be made.

I appreciate your immediate attention to this matter.
Regards,

Niccole Rogers, M.A.
Professional Merchandiser
Enclosure: 03/01/03 invoice, copy of contract terms

✳ ✳ ✳ ✳

Incorrect Payment

Niccole Rogers
P.O. Box 311573
Tampa, FL 33680
Tel. (813) 000-0000
Fax. (813) 000-0000
niccole@ncpmscenter.org

April 1, 2003

Great Merchandising Co.
Attention: Wanda Will
33 Anywhere Road
Anywhere, FL 33333
www.justshop.org
wanda@justshop.org

Re: Incorrect Payment

Dear Ms. Will:
On March 28, 2003, I received a check from your firm in the amount
of $50.00. Services were rendered as per your firm's instructions, and
my invoice correctly reflects the amount of $75.00 due.

Please issue payment for the remaining balance of $25.00 within the
next 5 business days. If payment will not be issued within the next 5
business days, please call or email me so arrangements can be made.

I appreciate your immediate attention to this matter.

Regards,

Niccole Rogers, M.A.
Professional Merchandiser

Enclosure: 03/01/03 invoice, copy of check, copy of contract terms

✳ ✳ ✳ ✳

Confirm an Assignment

Niccole Rogers
P.O. Box 311573
Tampa, FL 33680

Tel. (813) 000-0000
Fax. (813) 000-0000
niccole@ncpmscenter.org

April 1, 2003

Great Mystery Shopping Co.
Attention: Wanda Will
33 Anywhere Road
Anywhere, FL 33333

Dear Ms. Will:
Thank you for calling me. It is always a pleasure speaking with you.

I would like to take this opportunity to confirm the price and terms on the assignment issued March 1, 2003.

Assignment & Payment:
1. Debby's Delicious Diner @ Fowler Ave, $15.00 Flat Fee. Assignment will be completed on or before March 31, 2003.

2. Debby's Delicious Diner @ Bearss Ave, $15.00 Flat Fee. Assignment will be completed on or before March 31, 2003.

3. Debby's Delicious Diner @ 26th St, $15.00 Flat Fee. Assignment will be completed on or before March 31, 2003.

Payment will be rendered 15 days after a completed invoice has been faxed or mailed to your office.

Regards,

Niccole Rogers, M.A.
Professional Merchandiser

✳ ✳ ✳ ✳

Request to Use Your Name

Niccole Rogers
P.O. Box 311573
Tampa, FL 33680
Tel. (813) 000-0000
Fax. (813) 000-0000
niccole@ncpmscenter.org

April 1, 2003
Great Merchandising Co.
Attention: Wanda Will
33 Anywhere Road
Anywhere, FL 33333

Dear Ms. Will:

I would like to use your company name as a reference to verify my professional merchandising experience.

I have been a merchandising contractor with your firm for over three years and you are well known and respected in the professional merchandising community.

Please feel free to contact me on or before April 15, 2003, via email, fax or telephone if you would prefer that I not use your company name as a reference.

I appreciate your time and I look forward to working with you on future projects.

Sincerely,

Niccole Rogers, M. A.
Professional Merchandiser

✳ ✳ ✳ ✳

Change of Contact Information

If you are notifying companies via email, use this form.

> **SUBJECT: Change of Email Address for Niccole Rogers, Professional Shopper (effective immediately)**
>
> **Previous Contact Information:**
> **Niccole Rogers**
> **P.O. Box 311573, Tampa, FL 33680**
> **Tel. (813) 000-0000—Fax: (813) 000-0000**
> **Old Email: niccole@justshop.org**
>
> **New Contact Information:**
> **Niccole Rogers**
> **P.O. Box 311573, Tampa, FL 33680**
> **Tel. (813) 000-0000—Fax: (813) 000-0000**
> **New Email: niccole@ncpmscenter.org**

✳ ✳ ✳ ✳

Payment Request

> **Your Name Here**
> **Your Mailing Address Here**
> **Your Telephone Number Here**
>
> **Today's Date**
>
> **Business Name Here**
> **Business Mailing Address Here**
>
> **RE: Payment Request of $0.00**
>
> **Dear (Type Name Here): or To Whom It May Concern:**

My records indicate that I have not received payment for (print assignment name here). The assignment was completed on (print date here) and (snail mailed, emailed, faxed, called in) on (print date here).

If payment has been mailed or will be mailed within the next 5 business days, please excuse this letter. If payment has been denied or is not expected to be mailed within the next 5 business days, please provide the following information:

Payment is expected to be mailed by:
_____

Payment will not be mailed or has been denied because:
_____
_____

Completed assignment has been deemed unsatisfactory because:
_____

Thank you for taking the time to keep me up to date. If you have any questions, please feel free to contact me at the above address. I respectfully request a response to this letter within the next 5 business days.

I look forward to hearing from you.

Sign Your Name Here
Print Your Name Here
Your Assigned Identification Number Here
Enclosed: Proof of Delivered Assignment
Author: Niccole Rogers, M.A.

✳ ✳ ✳ ✳

Additional Organizational Tools

I frequently use a spreadsheet to organize the data on the companies I have contacted or work with. The column titles I use are:

Company name

Contact

Method of contact

Industry

Distribution frequency

User name

Password

Payment method

	Company Name	Contact	Method	Industry	User	Payment
1	Shop N Go	www.com	web	various	Star	fee + reim
2	Shop Head	phone		grocery	Star	fee
3	UShop	www.c	web	mall	Star	reimburse
4	We Shop	555-1111	phone	restaurant	Star	fee + reimburse
5						
6						
7						
8						
9						
10						
11						
12						
13						
14						

Another fantastic tool is located in the calendar section of your email. You can set up a daily recurring event and paste your contact list in the body of the event. Every day you will receive a notice with all your contact information. This is a fantastic method, for if you enter web sites it will automatically create links.

Next, I utilize a wall calendar to organize my travel. Let's say you schedule a day to visit a friend who lives an hour away. You can use the calendar to your advantage and respond to message board postings in this area. Now it is a business trip. Also, if you have a vacation coming, you do not want to schedule assignments 2 days before you leave, as you will be in a rush and will do a poor job. In addition, if the company requests follow-up information pertaining to the visit, you will not be available to respond, and the company may reassign the job.

The final tool I frequently use is a cupboard storage system. It is a tall wooden unit with several compartments. I have labeled the compartments *Monday, Tuesday, Wednesday, Thursday, Friday, Saturday* and *Sunday, next week*, and *next month*. This will assist you in organizing the abundance of paperwork you will receive pertaining to each assignment.

Taxes

Another common question I hear is, "Do I have to claim my earnings as income and pay taxes?" You are an independent contractor, and you are responsible for keeping accurate records. You must claim the income you make regardless of how many different companies you worked for. Individual companies that have paid you $600 or more will send you a Form 1099. Keep copies of all your receipts, and keep track of your mileage. These are all deductible. Consult your local tax professional for the specific laws in your state. If you net a total of $400, you must pay social security and Medicare only. If you net a total of $600 or more, you must also pay state and federal income tax. I strongly recommend that you report every penny, even if you operate at a loss. This is important because it will reduce your adjusted gross income, and you may receive additional funds back from the IRS for overpaying your taxes. For example, suppose your spouse made $15,000 in a given year and you operated at a $5,000 loss. Your combined taxable income is a total of $10,000, which will put you at a lower taxable income level and possibly prompt a refund.

You must report your self-employment income on Form 1040, Schedule C,—Profit or Loss From Business or on form 1040, Schedule C-EZ, Net Profit From Business. As a self-employed person, you pay your Medicare and social security taxes when you pay your income taxes, on Form 1040, Schedule SE, Self-Employment Tax. If you expect to owe $1,000 or more in income and self-employment taxes, you will need to make estimated tax payments. These payments are made quarterly using form 1040-ES, Estimated Tax for Individuals. You need to approximate these taxes at the beginning of the year. To learn about figuring and making estimated tax payments, please refer to Publication 505, Tax Withholding and Estimated Tax. (For the most current forms, please go to www.irs.gov; forms are available online for downloading).

The second most common question is, "What if I only want to do this as a hobby?" Well, the alternative for the hobby shopper is to keep a manual Schedule S running. At the end of the year, upon filing your taxes, you will be asked for the amount of income from a hobby as well as the total expenses for a hobby. However, if you net over $400, you will have to file a Schedule C and SE. Therefore, if you are serious about mystery shopping, you probably should use a Schedule C and start your business out on the right foot.

Tax Help

The following are helpful links that will focus your tax research.

Tax Terms
http://www.irs.ustreas.gov/prod/taxi/taxterms.html

Turbo Tax
http://www.turbotax.com/

Tax Links
http://www.taxlinks.com/

Online tax forms
http://www.irs.gov/forms_pubs/

Law Research
http://www.lawresearch.com/

The IRS (a great site)
http://www.irs.gov/

Deductible Items

A Schedule C, Profit or Loss From Business, has the following deductible items: advertising, bad debts from sales or services, car and truck expenses, commissions and fees, depletion, depreciation, employee benefit programs, insurance, mortgage, legal or professional services, office expense, pension or profit sharing, rent or lease (office or property), repairs and maintenance, supplies, taxes and licenses, travel (meals, entertainment, stipend), utilities, wages, and other. The following advice is merely that. The author is not a Certified Public Accountant, and it is your responsibility to consult an accountant or the IRS.

The number-one expense for a shopper is auto and travel, and there are several ways to claim vehicle usage. The most common is to claim 34.5 cents per mile and keep a mileage tracker in your vehicle. The rate per mile changes every year, so please consult your accountant or the IRS web site for the exact number. The next method is to compute a usage percentage for all expenses, consisting of but not limited to insurance, gas, car payments, and registration. For example, if you use the vehicle 80 percent of the time for business, you would total the expenses and compute 80 percent of the total as a business expense. The final way is to purchase or lease a company vehicle and write off all the expenses. However, if you do this, you may only use the vehicle for business purposes. Travel is a separate expense from auto and consists of airline tickets, hotels out of town, meals out of town, and other expenses such as tolls, cabs, and so on. So if you receive a hotel assignment, say, in San Diego, California, you may deduct your airline and cab expenses as business expenses. Therefore, you may want to treat yourself to a first-class ticket!

Some other categories are office expenses and utilities. Many small business owners opt to take the home office tax credit, which will be discussed later in the chapter. Other office expenses consist of, but are not limited to, paper, pencils, fax machine, ink cartridges, new computer, laptop, file folders, and software. Utility expenses consist of, but are not limited to, one-half of your current Internet connection, one-half of your basic phone bill (unless you acquire a business line—then your entire business phone), all business calls that are long distance, and possibly a business cell phone. The list of office expenses is unlimited, and you should take advantage of this deduction by supplying yourself with the best equipment and supplies. Remember, you are your own boss, so spoil yourself and purchase that comfortable chair you have been eyeing.

The next categories are insurance, employee benefits, and IRAs. You can purchase various types of insurance such as health, life, or disability, as a small business owner and claim it as either a business expense or a personal expense. I recommend notifying your auto insurance company of the business usage of your vehicle. Some companies will charge you an additional $50 per year, but you are being honest and not opening yourself up to various loopholes in your auto insurance contract. Additionally, the increased amount is deductible as a business expense. You may also open tax shelter accounts such as an IRA and have the company match the amount invested. The amount matched by the company is considered a business expense, and the personal investment in the IRA is deducted before the gross taxes are calculated.

Another category is called professional development. This category is important because you can deduct any seminars or classes you take pertaining to small businesses or taxes. Additionally, you may deduct the cost of this book or this course, for had you not purchased this book or taken this course, you would not have a new career.

Many students inquire about the home office tax credit. The credit may be up to $5,000 per year. However, do not be misled about the nature of this tax credit. Because you are claiming a portion of your home as an office, when you sell your home, you are selling office property and have to claim that as equity; thus, you must repay all the credits you had previously taken. This tax credit is very deceiving, and I personally would not recommend it. My suggestion is that you not take this credit or consult with your tax accountant as to what is most beneficial to your situation.

The last category is reimbursed business expenses, and it is the most confusing to new shoppers or recovering accountants. Let's discuss a grocery store assignment. Most grocery assignments require you to make a purchase of around $5, for which you are reimbursed, and then pay you an additional fee of $20 for completion of the assignment. If you did not make the $5 purchase, you would not be able to complete the assignment because the purchase is a requirement. Therefore, the $5 purchase is a reimbursed business expense and is not taxable. Additionally, you get to keep the product tax free. Please review the following calculations.

Payment	$25.00
Expense	$ 5.00
Net	$20.00

The gross payment or income received before deductions is $25, and the net payment or income received after deductions is $20.

Let us take a look at a Schedule C chart for additional clarity.

Gross	$15,000
Reimbursed business expense	$ 7,000
Utilities	$ 2,000
Mileage	$ 3,400
Insurance	$ 1,000
Travel	$ 2,000
Office expenses	$ 2,000
Net	-$2,000

Your gross income is $15,000, yet on the books you made a negative $2,000, so it appears that you are operating at a loss. Therefore, you pay zero taxes! This is a good thing, because although you may appear to be operating at a loss, what did you do? You traveled, stayed at hotels, ate some wonderful meals, and deducted numerous expenses for things you would have been doing anyway, and you may even get a tax refund! I assure you, you will not always operate at a loss; however, it is perfectly legal to operate at a loss as long as you are making an honest attempt to operate at a profit. Most businesses, especially small businesses, operate at a loss the first 2 years. The government used to red-flag those that operated at a loss the third year. This is no longer the case, however. I recommend that you be honest about your efforts, claim every penny earned, and file your taxes honestly and accurately each year.

SS-4 Instructions

The most important thing to remember about filling out the SS-4 is that if you elect to choose a company name or DBA, you must obtain a business license and request property zoning for a home office from your city and state. Additionally, your accounting method should be cash and your closing month December so that you can file your business taxes with your personal taxes. You can file for your EIN either by mail, phone or fax, or online. Once you receive an EIN you can use it in lieu of your Social Security Number.

IRS

6271 Box 9941, Ogden, UT 84201

Phone: (800) 829-4933

Fax: (801) 620-7115

Online: https://sa2.www4.irs.gov/sa_vign/newFormSS4.do

Please visit www.irs.gov for additional or updated information. Please visit http://www.irs.gov/pub/irs-pdf/iss4.pdf for specific instructions pertaining to the completion of an SS-4 form.

Schedule C Instructions

Schedule C is the form for reporting profit or loss from a business. You will need to complete this form at the end of every year and file it with your 1040 personal taxes. There are several main things to remember, such as whether your company is a cash-based company, with assets and liabilities being recorded as they occur. In other words, you enter an expense or money received on the day the transaction takes place. You will not amortize or claim any type of depreciation. I will discuss pertinent line items on the form, and the form is available in the appendix for viewing.

Line 9: Bad debt. You can write off short payments to bad debt.

Line 10: Vehicle expense. See "Deductible Items" earlier in the chapter.

Line 14: Employee benefit programs: You may set up a health, dental, and optical plan through your company.

Line 15: Insurance. You can deduct expenses such as an increase in insurance due to business use. Additionally, I purchased laptop insurance for $50 a year. If the laptop is stolen or broken, it will be replaced with a modern version.

Line 16: Interest. You may place your credit card interest expense in this area. For example, if you use your credit card for assignment and accrue interest, it is a business expense.

Line 17: Professional and legal services. If you hire an accountant, you may place the expense here.

Line 18: Office expense. Lines 18 and 22 are fairly interchangeable, covering items such as fax machines, chairs, computers, paper, printer, pens, and so on.

Line 19: Pension and profit sharing. You can set up a pension plan.

Line 21: Repairs. You can place office maintenance items in this area, such as costs incurred if your computer crashes or needs repair.

Line 22: Supplies. See line 18.

Line 23: Taxes and licenses. Any fees you have paid for a business license or a private investigator's license plus prior year business taxes.

Line 24: Travel. Any travel expenses may be placed in this area, such as rental cars, airline tickets, tolls, meals, sundries, and entertainment.

Line 25: Utilities. You may write off half of your basic phone expense plus any long distance calls. If you purchase a separate phone line, then you may deduct the entire expense. Additionally, you can include half of the cost of your Internet access.

Line 27: Other expenses. Page 2 has an area for computing your vehicle miles plus an area for other expenses. In this area, you may include expenses such as reimbursed business expenses, postage, professional development, and so on.

Remember, you must include your reimbursed business expenses in your gross income or in other income.

You must report every penny you earn as a mystery shopper, even if your business operates at a loss and even if you complete only one assignment!

For current procedures and instructions pertaining to Schedule C, please visit http://www.irs.gov/pub/irs-pdf/i1040sc.pdf.

Tax Information

SS-4—for employer identification number
Fax: (801) 620-7115
IRS, 6271 Box 9941, Ogden, UT 84201

Online instructions
http://www.irs.gov/businesses/small/article/0,,id=102767,00.
html

Document
https://sa2www4irs.gov/sa_vign/newFormSS4.do

Payment

There are three payment methods: reimbursement only, flat fee, and reimbursement plus a fee. Family restaurants and hotels are typically reimbursement only assignments. The restaurant assignments will have a cap of usually around $50, and you will be asked to bring two to four people. Hotels are unique in that you can pick any size room, such as the Deluxe Honeymoon Suite for $300, and receive full reimbursement. These assignments are great family activities that can increase your quality of life or prompt you to take an overnight vacation. The next method is reimbursement plus a fee; this is the most common payment method. Industries such as restaurants, gas stations, retail stores, and grocery stores typically use this method. You will be asked to make a small purchase and will be paid an additional fee. For example, a grocery store assignment will require you to make a $5 purchase, and in addition you will receive a flat fee of $20. You need to note that the $5 is a reimbursed business expense, for if you had not made this purchase, you could not have completed the assignment. Thus, the $20 is your net profit. The last category is the flat fee; examples of businesses using this method are car dealerships, apartments, cell phone stores, and other retail stores. You will not be asked to rent an apartment or purchase a car, instead, you will be asked to evaluate the presentation and overall environment of the facility, and you will be paid a flat fee.

Next, the average industry payment terms are *net 60*, which means that you will not be paid for 2 *months* after completing the assignment. This is important, because if you stay at a luxury hotel and you have a rather large bill, you will have to pay the interest on your credit card bill twice before you receive payment. The interest is tax deductible, but you may want to start out small and with locations that you would be visiting normally, such as the grocery store or pet store. It is not mandatory to mystery-shop an expensive hotel and spend a major amount of money. So I encourage you to test the waters and decide which type of assignment you are comfortable with. Try a few of each type of assignment and see what fits. For example, I will no longer mystery-shop car dealerships, for I find them to be too humbling and not very cost effective.

The final and most frequently asked question is, "How much will I actually make?" Well, this depends on the assignments you accept. You will not make a penny if you accept reimbursement only restaurant and hotel assignments, but you will have a great time and a bunch of tax

deductions. However, if you operate as a mystery shopper full-time, you can make about $40,000 per year. Now this is functioning as a shopper 8 hours a day, 5 days a week. I strongly recommend shopping only as a part-time contractor, for you may experience shopper burn out. For example, imagine visiting 10 grocery stores a day 5 days a week. You would make about $1,000 a week, but it doesn't sound like much fun. Below is a list of various assignments and the average pricing.

Assignment	Average Pricing ($)	Hours
Apartments	15–40	1–3
Appliance/stereo	8–20	1/2
Auto dealerships	50–75	1–3
Auto supply	8–20	1/2
Banks—financial management	45–55	1–2
Banks—teller and new accounts	15–30	1/2–1
Casinos	75–150	2–3
Cell phone	10–15	1/2
Clothing	8–50	1
Convenience stores	8–10	1/4
Cruise lines	Reimbursement to 1,000	24–168
Department stores	10–50	1
Electronics stores	8–20	1/2

Family dining	Reimbursement only	2
Fast food	8–15	15–30
Fine fining	150–250	2–4
Florists	45–100	1
Gas stations	8–10	1/4
Grocery stores	10–25	1
Hardware	8 – 20	1/2
Hotels	Reimbursement only	24
Hotels—four-star	250–3,000	24–168
Movie theaters	10–50	1/2 – 6
New home construction	50–150	3
Night clubs	25–200	2–3
Office supplies	8–20	1/2–1
Pet stores	8–20	1/2
Quick lube	Reimbursement only	1/2–1
Specialty shops	8–20	1/2
Theme parks	Reimbursement to 100	24– 48
Toy stores	8–20	1/2
Travel agents	15–30	1

Finally, you will need to figure the actual hourly rate for each assignment, taking into account driving distance, shop time, and reporting time. For example, if you accept an assignment at a grocery store 45 miles away, it will take you 2 hours to drive to and from the location, plus 30 minutes in the location and 20 minutes to write the report, giving a total of 3 hours to complete the process. This comes out to about $6.50 per hour for a grocery store assignment that pays approximately $25. So please make sure that you do these calculations and are at least making above minimum wage!

Problems with Payment

If you are concerned about unethical companies where others have had issues about getting paid, then I suggest viewing the following web sites:

NCPMS

www.justshop.org/bizcheck.htm

Undercover Shoppers

http://groups.msn.com/UndercoverShoppers/companyfeedback.
   msnw

In addition, if you need assistance with a difficult or hostile situation, please contact the NCPMS. The NCPMS offers free mediation and litigation services. The web site is www.justshop.org

Paypal

Paypal is an electronic payment system similar to ADP. If you trust the ADP as a direct deposit agency then you will love Paypal. Many companies that have online scheduling utilize the Paypal system for making payments to shoppers. First you must sign up for Paypal at https:// www.paypal.com; it is of course, free. Paypal will place $5 in your bank account as a welcome and also to ensure that the process is working. After you complete an assignment, the contracting company will send you a notice that you have been paid via Paypal. You will receive a notice from Paypal as well. You then visit the Paypal web site, and you have the opportunity to have a physical check mailed to you or to have the funds deposited directly into your checking account. You may also spend the money online or send gift certificates to others. The site is very secure and is federally regulated as well as monitored.

Benefits

There are many benefits that one can acquire when one enters the field of mystery shopping. These benefits have been discussed in detail throughout the book and consist of improving the quality of service in the community, finding good locations to frequent or recommend, getting paid to research a product, small business tax write-offs, having your opinion acknowledged—or simply the money!

Mystery shopping is not the easiest job in the world; however, it is by my definition one of the most fun! You are basically being paid to do things you would normally be doing, and it will definitely enhance your quality of life. I encourage you to take hotel assignments out of town and work on your laptop at the pool while enjoying a margarita—all the while thinking, I am going to get paid for this.

סוגיה

International Opportunities

M ystery shopping has expanded all over the world, and opportunities do exist internationally. However, you must make yourself aware of the current international tax laws. Additionally, shoppers are not typically reimbursed for travel expenses; however, these expenses are deductible on form Schedule C under travel expenses. Therefore, you can easily turn an expensive vacation into a deductible business trip with the acquisition of one international assessment or assignment.

You may want to consider the payment as well. If you are paid by a company that is located in another country, you may be paid in a different currency, and the currency rate may fluctuate. For example, on one occasion I was paid in British pounds instead of U.S. dollars, and as a result the payment was about half of the agreed amount. Furthermore, your bank may charge a conversion fee or an international processing fee for a foreign check.

Publication 54 describes in detail what a shopper must pay if he or she works abroad. Essentially the taxes are the same; however, each situation is different. To view Publication 54, please visit the following site:

http://www.irs.gov/pub/irs-pdf/p54.pdf.

Canada is one exception to the rule. If you mystery shop in Canada, you may be subject to double taxation by both Canada and the

United States. Please visit the following Canadian tax sites for more information:

http://www.ccra-adrc.gc.ca/menu-e.html

http://www.ccra-adrc.gc.ca/E/pub/tg/rc4110/rc4110ed.html

Company Listings and Other International Links

The following are international links that will focus your search for international assignments.

Australia

http://www.mysteryshopper.com.au/

http://www.hoedholdings.com.au/

http://www.aamerch.com/

UK companies

http://www.nop.co.uk/mystery/hp_mystery.shtml

http://www.mystery-shoppers.co.uk

http://www.performanceinpeople.co.uk

http://www.pigservices.co.uk

http://www.bpri.co.uk/CRM.html

http://www.networkhg.org.uk/data/solon-network/data/mystery-shopping.htm

http://www.aba.co.uk

http://www.macphersonmysteryshopping.org.uk

http://www.virtuoso.maritzresearch.com

http://ourworld.cs.com/precsresch/PRIweb/

http://www.homeworkinguk.com/mystery.htm

Mystery-Shopping List of Companies and Organizations

http://dmoz.org/Business/Customer_Service/Mystery_Shopping/

Information on International Mystery-Shopping—Lazy Cat Surveys

http://www.geocities.com/lazycatsurveys/mystery_shopping.html

List of 34 International Mystery Shopping Companies

http://www.worldmall.tv/mystery_shopping_directory.htm#International%20Companies

MSPA—(Sorted by Country)

http://www.mysteryshop.org/europe/shoppers.php

Volition

http://www.volition.com/mysteryint.html

Canadian Message Lists for Leads

CAN-MysteryShops@yahoogroups.com
CanShop@yahoogroups.com
mychc4u@yahoogroups.com

CHAPTER 12

Summing It Up

The occupation of mystery shopping is like no other. You will be paid to do things you would normally be doing, and then some. Assignments consist of, but are not limited to, establishments and activities such as grocery stores, gas stations, carpet cleaners, dry cleaners, hotels, fine dining, oil changes, and much, much more! I have a newfound freedom in the occupation of mystery shopping, as it provides me with the option to accept or decline each activity of my day. If the assignment is not a good match or if it is too far, I can say no, and in that act there is great pleasure.

Organizations and Assistance

The assistance does not end with the completion of this book. There are many organizations designed with one goal: to help you, the shopper, succeed. Additionally, I am always a source.

Serving Mystery Shoppers, Merchandisers, Companies, and Groups

The National Center for Professional Mystery Shoppers, Inc. (NCPMS) is an organization made up of shoppers for shoppers. The site offers leads, newsletters, forms, free legal advice, online courses, and certification. It can be reached at http://www.justshop.org/ and www.ncpmscenter.org.

The Mystery Shopping Providers Association (MSPA) is an organization made up of mystery-shopping companies whose purpose is to establish unity and ethical standards in the industry. It has a great site for researching mystery-shopping companies by a specific industry, state, or even country. Additionally, it is a great source for inquiring about the legitimacy of an organization. So before you invest in a high-end hotel assignment, you may want to contact the MSPA. It can be reached at http://www.mysteryshop.org/.

Here are some other useful sites:

International Association of Service Evaluators (IASE)—Serving Mystery-Shopping Providers, www.iasemysteryshop.com

National Association for Retail Marketers (NARMS)—Serving Merchandising Providers, www.narms.com

Marketing Research Association (MRA)—Serving Mystery-Shopping Providers, www.mra-net.org

National Association for Self-Employed (NASE), www.nase.org

Women Inc.com, www.womeninc.com

Work-at-Home Mothers (AWAHM), www.awahm.org

American Business Women (ABWA), www.abwahq.org

Association of Business Support Services International (ABSSI), www.abssi.org

Digital-Women, www.digital-women.com

NCPMS and Mediation

The NCPMS does offer peer mediation. Both parties must agree to participate in the mediation. The mediation is not legally binding. You can, however, ask the second party to agree (by contract) to legally uphold the final decision.

Look over the helpful hints below. If you would like the NCPMS to act as a mediator, send an email at ncpms@ncpmscenter.org. You must try to resolve the situation using the methods below; if you do not succeed, the volunteer peer mediation process will begin.

1. Attempt to speak to a company representative about your problem on five to seven separate occasions. Keep a detailed log of

your phone calls, emails, and faxes. It is important that you keep track of all interactions from this date forward. Do not use a company's 800 number. You need to use a number that will show on your long distance bill. These phone calls will confirm your attempts to make contact with the company. If the company is local, use your cellular phone to make the call. The call will be logged on your monthly itemized cellular billing statement.

2. Each and every time you interact with this company, send an email, fax, or certified letter with return receipt to confirm the interaction. The letter should include the date, time, people included in the conversation, and a summary of the conversation.

3. Keep a copy of everything that is faxed, emailed or mailed.

4. Formally request payment. Write the company a certified letter with a delivery and return receipt. In the letter, you want to request payment. It is very important that your message be courteous and straight to the point. Leave your personal feelings out of it.

Include a copy of your phone summaries, all emails, fax receipts, and mailed receipts. In your letter, you want to request a response within 7 to 10 business days after the letter has been received.

5. If the company has a fax machine, fax all the information listed in the previous item. Be sure to save the confirmation page showing that your documents were actually sent to the company. You also want to send the documents via U.S. mail with a return receipt.

6. Now is the time to research other options. In case the problem is not resolved or you do not receive a response, prioritize your options in the order in which you intend to seek services.

Obtain the number for your state labor department in case you need to file a complaint.

Research mediation services available in your city or county.

Contact Niccole at NCPMS, ncpms@ncpmscenter.org, about the problem.

Research information on filing a small claims suit in your city or county.

Check with your local Better Business Bureau to see if it accepts complaints involving contract disputes.

Search the Web to see if anyone else has had any problems with the company.

7. If the company does not respond, send another letter (certified with return receipt) explaining that you have not heard from the company and that you will use your city and state resources to collect payment. Request that the company respond within 3 business days. Again send the company a copy of the material listed in item 4.

8. If the company does does not respond or refuses payment, use the options that you have researched in item 6.

Remember, do not make statements or comments that you do not intend to follow through on. Making threats or using methods to intimidate when you do not plan to follow through reduces the overall effect that the comments were designed to have. If you plan to file a small claims suit, do it!

It is also important to remember that you can resolve an issue faster by remaining professional. Remember, the company still has your money! Sending threats and demands often puts people on the defensive. You want to work with the company to resolve the issue. No matter what, you want to always remain calm and professional.

More Helpful Hints

Always keep a detailed log of your contacts with the company from the beginning until the situation is completely resolved. That includes emails, telephone calls, faxes, and any mailed correspondence.

Always remain professional, in your tone of voice and your correspondence. Make sure your letters are always courteous. Do not make letters personal—keep your contact strictly professional and businesslike. This is not about your personal feelings; this is about business and collecting payment.

Do not let time lapse when resolving conflict. The other party will not consider your complaint serious if you are not consistent.

Decide right now if your complaint is serious. If you are trying to recover $15, that does not qualify as serious. Please just write it off as a bad debt on your Schedule C at the end of the year. I guarantee that

$15 is not worth your time, as you will spend twice that amount trying to receive payment.

Do not make threats or demands. Simply tell the company your position and what you intend to do to resolve the complaint. Always make it seem as though you are on the company's side and are not out to cause problems—but you want to resolve the existing dispute.

If you make a statement that explains your intention of taking action, it is imperative that you follow through. Scare tactics are not taken seriously, and we have all heard them before. So if you make such a statement, follow through.

Here are web sites you can use to inquire about a company's status in the community:

forums.delphiforums.com/justshop/start

http://www.justshop.org/bizcheck.htm

Related Industries

A market research organization may offer additional services to clients and may contact you to perform these services. These services include merchandising, auditing, demonstrating, interviewing, business verifications, trailers, mail tracking, and tele-checks. Merchandising involves setting up a display or stocking a product, which may be anything from 12-packs of Pepsi to greeting cards. An auditor is someone who reviews the work of the merchandiser. You simply enter the store and note whether the display is visible and the items are stocked. A demonstrator is usually described as someone who hands out free samples and coupons. Next is the interviewer, or the person at the mall who tries to stop you for a survey. The business verification assignment is specific to real estate rental property; you are to make an appointment with the manager to view the location of the credit report system. Basically, you are noting on a survey if the credit report system is secure and not accessible to the public. The e-jury.com is an online trial and jury project initiated by several lawyers in Arizona. You must register, and then you will be matched with a case. The case for both sides will be presented including various data and pictures. You will be asked to rule as if you were a member of a jury, indicating how much compensation you would allow and what the determining factors were that led you to your decision. A trailer is a movie preview and is a very fun assignment. You simply enter the theater and ask to speak with the manager. You state that you are there to complete a trailer check, and the manager allows you and a guest in for free. In the theater you note whether the audience reacted to the movie previews in a positive or a negative manner, then you are free to watch the movie. Mail checks are also a lot of fun. You sign up with a company that mails information to an alias name at your home. You simply enter the information from the letter, magazine, or flyer online at the company web site and are paid 25 cents for each piece of mail. I receive subscriptions to many magazines for free, and I get paid a quarter to record each item. Finally, a tele-check is a mystery-shopping phone call that is recorded. This is a wonderful assignment for disabled people and women who are 9 months pregnant or have just given birth and have difficulty leaving the home.

Serving Merchandising Companies

Below are the leading merchandising organizations that can jump-start your career as a merchandiser.

NARMS

http://www.narms.com/

MRA

http://www.mra-net.org

Industry Changes

The industry is starting to change slightly in terms of technology and fee reduction. A few companies are now requiring a shopper to obtain a digital camera or video equipment. Ironically, these are the companies that pay very minimal fees, such as $10 to $15 for digital images and a combination report more than three pages long. I highly recommend declining these types of assignments, for I consider some of the companies to be borderline abusive to their shoppers.

In order to be successful as a full-time mystery shopper who receives high-end assignments, it is essential that you become computer literate. Many of the high-end assignments require fluency in Excel, Word, and the World Wide Web. Although it is not necessary to be computer literate to receive mystery shops, becoming educated in computer software will certainly improve your career and your earning power as a mystery shopper.

For several types of high-end assignments, the shopper is now required to record certain transactions via audiotape or video camera. Some shoppers purchase a lapel microphone to hide the recording device. However, companies that require hidden video recordings typically supply the shopper with the equipment. Many shoppers have asked me about the legalities of recording an employee. Most companies that utilize this type of assessment require employees to sign a waiver stating that they are aware that they may be recorded via audiotape or video camera for evaluation and training purposes.

Scams

A new Internet paradigm is occurring that I consider to be a scam. It mainly involves a few scheduling agencies. They are setting up web sites and asking shoppers to register for a fee; however, the fee is unstated and the shopper is asked to provide credit card information upon registration. Therefore, the scheduling companies receive payments from the shoppers as well as from the contracting companies simply by having a web site. Please be aware of this type of scam and be advised that there are over 750 mystery-shopping companies that would love to have you on board and pay you generously as well as treat you with honor and respect.

The next type of unethical organization is the list broker. Such a company will copy or compile a list of mystery-shopping agencies and will gladly sell you the list for approximately $40, payable by credit card, cash, or cashier's check . These proposals are usually made via spam mail or in the newspaper. One is merely purchasing a list of companies and receives no other guidance on business law or industry components.

Another scam involves employment agencies. They will place an ad in a local newspaper for mystery shoppers and will pay $8 to 10 per hour for assignments that they receive $25 to 50 for completing. in addition, they will take taxes out of your check, and you will be asked to use your own vehicle and pay for gas. This is a winning situation for the employment agency and a losing situation for you as a shopper. You can acquire these assignments on your own if you let it be known that you are interested in shopping.

Finally, a rule of thumb is, if someone is asking for money, it is a scam. One example is to ask for a processing or registration fee for your application. Now, if you were to apply to work at a local McDonald's, would the company ask for a processing fee? So please do not consider paying any additional fees whatsoever, for all the information I provided to you in this book offers links and resources that are available to you at no cost.

Schedulers

A scheduler is a private agency that receives funding from a mystery shopping company to match shoppers to assignments. It has come to my attention that several scheduling organizations are demanding additional fees from shoppers in order to receive preferential treatment. This is not a standard or ethical business practice. Never pay a scheduler for an assignment or for preferential treatment.

Scaling

Scaling is the term used to describe the passing of mystery-shopping programs to various companies in order to reduce the cost of the program. For example, an assignment enters the industry as offering reimbursement plus a payment of $100. The market research agency is then outbid by another company that claims it can provide more information at a lower cost. The assignment is then reduced to $75 plus reimbursement. The bidding process continues, and results eventually in the shopper's being offered $5 plus reimbursement with a 10-page form to complete. Do not accept assignments that will result in your abuse. You want to make more than minimum wage!

Shopper's Remorse

This occurs when a shopper has experienced the pleasures of an assignment and now must process the data. We are typically used to working at a job, receiving the funds, and then purchasing our joy. It is difficult to adjust to experiencing the joy prior to doing the work. For example, a shopper will commit to a fine dining or resort experience. He or she enjoys the visit and now must record the data. The shopper does not want to record the data because he or she did not realize how difficult the work can be. He or she then decides not to complete the work because it is "too hard," and is thus left with the expense. Remember, you must enjoy both people and paperwork to succeed in this industry. It is work, but it is the best job you will ever love!

Final Words of Caution

Always remember to ask questions before committing to an assignment. If the company is hesitant to provide answers, do not work with it. Also ask what the fee is, what the location is, what the due date and time frame are, and what the turnaround time is —2 hours or 2 days. Remember to get everything in writing prior to engaging in an assignment, especially the fee. If the data do not include the financial parameters, contact the company immediately and ask for this information in writing via fax or email. Finally, do not overcommit. Do not accept 10 grocery stores because they are offered to you. Ask for the locations and accept two. Be sure not to overcommit until you absolutely know that this industry is for you.

Designing Your Goals

Now that you have been thoroughly educated in the field of mystery shopping, you must design your personal goals. You must ask yourself the following questions:

Do you want to shop full-time, part-time, or as a hobby?

Do you plan to travel as a shopper?

How much time do you have available?

How often do you want to shop?

What types of assignments interest you?

Would you excel with questionnaires or narrative forms?

How much money do you want to make as a shopper?

Certification

The NCPMS and MSPA are the only two organizations that actually certify shoppers. They are also the largest mystery-shopping training providers in the United States. I think both organizations have excellent programs. The method, delivery, and content may differ, but the goal is similar. They both want to strengthen and uplift the industry.

Why Is the NCPMS a Great Choice?

The NCPMS serves approximately 10,000 companies, schedulers, and contractors annually.

It's membership (companies, schedulers, and contractors) numbers 4,706.

The NCPMS has served 89 percent of all recognized mystery-shopping companies (approximately 600 companies).

There are 326 mystery-shopping and merchandising companies that acknowledge NCPMS certifications.

The NCPMS formally mediates 12 to 22 cases per year.

It is the first national organization to offer this level of training to shoppers and merchandisers.

The organization trained 528 shoppers in 2002.

It has highly trained and talented instructors who hold a variety of professional memberships and certifications.

What Is Certification?

By definition, a certificate is an affirmation. It testifies that something has occurred or will occur. The governing body that issues the certification has the ability to create reserved rights. The governing body usually states that when a problem arises with any certification, it reserves the right to suspend and/or revoke that certification. The words *suspend* and *revoke* usually indicate that the certification is temporarily or permanently disabled or no longer recognized because the governing body can no longer testify on that individual's behalf.

What Do I Get for $39.95?

For $39.95, a shopper or merchandiser will get:

- Three certified online workshops
- Generic continuing education units (CEU)
- Free refresher workshops
- Certification from a national organization
- Training by experienced instructors
- A forum for interacting with peers

If I Have Taken Some of the Required Workshops at Another School, Do I Need to Take Them Again?

No. You can transfer in credits from other schools and training centers if you have taken and successfully completed relevant courses, workshops, or seminars with an 87 percent or higher grade. The NCPMS Learning Center accepts credits from:

- NARMS
- MSPA
- Any university or college

- Brain Bench.com
- 247University.com
- Any vendor who meets or exceeds the mystery-shopping and merchandising national education standards

What Is a Seasoned Contractor?

A seasoned contractor is an individual who has successfully completed more than 100 mystery-shopping or merchandising assignments or has been active in the industry for more than 3 years.

Why 100 Assignments or 3 Years?

Based on our experience and interaction with contractors, NCPMS believes that any contractor who has completed 100 assignments or has been an active mystery shopper or merchandiser for 3 years is more likely than not to be knowledgeable about different assignment types, industry terms, ethics, basic math, and other basic business skills.

The NCPMS also believes (based on experience) that any contractor who has this particular knowledge will conduct business in a much more professional manner, which leads to less conflict.

I Am a Seasoned Contractor; How Do I Get Started?

If you are a seasoned contractor (see the definition), please email Niccole@ncpmscenter.org to register. After you have completed your registration, the NCPMS will request an up-to-date résumé. The NCPMS will also send you a quick review packet to help you prepare for the Knowledge and Skill Set Test. When your résumé (and other requested information, if applicable) has been returned and you are ready to take the test, the NCPMS will give you access to the test.

What if I Just Want to Take the Test?

You may skip the online or local workshops and go straight to the Knowledge and Skill Set Test (KASST) if you meet one of the following conditions:

- You are a seasoned contractor.
- You are MSPA Gold Certified.
- You have completed the relevant NARMS course and certification.
- You have completed the relevant university or college courses.
- You have completed relevant Brain Bench courses.
- You have completed relevant 247University courses.
- You have completed mystery-shopping or merchandising work-shops or seminars by vendors who meet or exceed the National Education Committee standards.

What Is the Knowledge and Skill Set Test (KASST)?

The Knowledge and Skill Set Test is a comprehensive exam designed to test and verify knowledge and skill in the areas of contractor expertise, conducting business, and advanced communication. All contractors taking the test must receive an 87 percent or higher score in order to pass.

What If I Am Nervous about Taking the Test?

Do not be nervous. A review guide and sample test are included in this book to help you prepare. You also have the option of taking an online workshop that will help you bring your current knowledge and skills up to date.

What Is a Free Refresher Workshop?

A refresher workshop is an online or local workshop designed to cover additional business skills. Here are a few examples of topics:

- Customer service
- Mediation
- Goal setting
- Measuring performance
- Financial planning

Can You Promise That I Will Get Jobs After I Am Certified?

Absolutely *not*! No reputable school or training center will promise you a job without knowing where you live, your availability, or how many contracts are active in your area.

After I Get Certified, Can I Just Sit Back and Let the Jobs Roll In?

Absolutely *not*! This is the biggest mistake new contractors make.

Certification can open doors for independent contractors. However, independent contractors are responsible for building and maintaining professional and productive relationships that lead to career advancement.

When Does the Certification Expire?

Certification expires in 2 years. All certified contractors will have the opportunity to renew their certification before it expires. In order to renew, a participant must complete 5 clock hours of training over a 2-year period. Training can be delivered in the form of a chat, class, seminar, workshop, or volunteering.

I Already Have Contracts; Do I Really Need to Get Certified?

No, it is not necessary for any mystery shopper or merchandiser to get certified at this time. However, seasoned shoppers or merchandisers (full-time or part-time) need to show some level of growth throughout their career.

Can My Company Pay for My Training?

Absolutely! There are a number of companies that offer paid training for their independent contractors and employees. Contact your company representative for details.

How Does This Program Compare
to the MSPA Certification?

It is recommended that that you print out both programs and highlight the pros and cons of each. Based on that information, determine which program will meet your short- and long-term goals.

You have the following options:

• Do not pursue certification.

• Pursue MSPA certification.

• Pursue NCPMS certification.

• Pursue both MSPA and NCPMS certification.

Why Do So Few Companies Request
an NCPMS Certification Number?

The certification was just released in August 2003.

The NCPMS continues to work with over 600 mystery-shopping and merchandising companies. Each company will (and should with NCPMS full support) use and accept the certification at its discretion according to the contracts negotiated with its current and future clients.

The NCPMS provides specialized training for a number of companies. Now that they are certifying contractors, this information will automatically be updated in the requesting company's database.

Do Companies Actually
Recognize This Certification?

Yes. I answer this question reluctantly because I want to make sure that contractors focus on the education first. I want contractors to understand how important it is for them to invest in themselves and their career. There are some companies that recognize NCPMS certification. Certainly not all companies do, and MSPA members probably do not, since they have their own program.

How Does This Course Compare to the MSPA's?

The two organizations (NCPMS and MSPA) have similar goals. The delivery and content in some cases may vary. The MSPA does not recognize or accept NCPMS certification, as the NCPMS is not a member.

Again, the NCPMS suggests that you review both programs and see which one will help you meet your short- and long-term goals.

Why Should I Have to Pay So Much for Certification If I Do Not Need to Take the Courses?

The fee covers the continual rewriting that is necessary to keep the test up to date. Also, refresher courses are free to certified contractors; however, the NCPMS still needs to pay the instructors. Certified contractors can take as many refresher courses as they are able to handle.

Do You Provide Specialized Services for Contractors with Disabilities?

Absolutely. The NCPMS provides the test (KASST) via telephone.

What Are Relevant University or College Courses?

The NCPMS accepts any classes that have something to do with basic business functions, business management, leadership, and/or English, such as:

- Accounting
- Economics
- Management
- Business law

- Strategic planning
- Business communication
- Conflict resolution

In short, the NCPMS needs to be able to verify that you have the knowledge to conduct a secret shopping/merchandising business in a professional manner.

NCPMS Online Learning Center Policies and Procedures

www.ncpmscenter.org

www.justshop.org

The NCPMS Online Learning Center policies and procedures cover culture, confidentiality, ethics, payments, responsibilities, and code of conduct expectations.

By accepting the classroom screen name and password or registering with the NCPMS Learning Center, participants acknowledge that they fully understand and agree to uphold the policies and procedures here. The NCPMS is dedicated to providing quality training and education and the following policies are taken very seriously.

Culture

The NCPMS Learning Center strongly believes that contractors and employees should value and embrace the opportunity to learn and sharpen their skills.

Participants and instructors actively engage and grow by sharing their knowledge and expertise. All participants agree to fully participate in online workshop activities, and actively engage in online discussions. Participation is needed to make each workshop fun and rewarding. Any person(s) who does not participate will be removed from the workshop.

The NCPMS Learning Center supports and provides the tools for a wide range of learning and growth activities. As a learning center that services the entire mystery-shopping and merchandising community, we encourage

- **Opinions and ideas**
- **Constructive feedback**
- **Active participation in the growth process**

- New strategy development
- Respect and civility
- Stimulating debates
- Goal-centered learning
- Self-assessments

Workshop/Classroom Confidentiality

All identities, materials, ideas, views, discussions, and information that is located or originates in the NCPMS Online Learning Center is strictly confidential and shall not be used without the author(s) written permission. All current and former participants and instructors shall uphold and respect this online workshop/classroom confidentiality statement.

Ethics

All participants will feel free to learn and share their ideas. The NCPMS Online Learning Center demonstrates respect for Participants and Instructors.

Payments

Participants agree to pay any fees including the price of the workshop before the workshop is complete (unless other payment arrangements have been made).

Responsibilities

It is both the responsibility of the instructor and the participant to:

- Have fun.
- Keep the learning center free of unrelated materials.
- Fully engage in the online workshop/classroom activities.
- Uphold the online workshop/classroom ethics and code of conduct.
- Respect and support workshop/classroom confidentiality.
- Report any harassing or unwelcome behavior to the instructor and Niccole Rogers.
- Contact Niccole Rogers when your expectations are not being met.

Instructors have added responsibilities, including

- Promoting and maintaining a fruitful learning environment
- Providing adequate and sufficient feedback to all participants
- Reporting unengaged participants

Code of Conduct Expectations

All participants and instructors will actively engage in online workshops/classrooms a minimum of four times per week. A week is defined as Monday through Sunday.

All participants and instructors will respect and uphold the NCPMS Online Learning Center's culture, confidentiality, responsibilities, ethics and code of conduct expectations.

All participants and instructors will provide timely feedback to preserve the online learning structure and experience.

Unacceptable Conduct

- Sharing any materials, ideas, identities, views, or discussions that originate in the NCPMS Online Learning Centers is strictly prohibited and violates workshop/classroom confidentiality.

- Misrepresenting personal identities, educational experience, ideas, materials, or views is a deliberate distraction and is not acceptable.

- Violating copyright infringement laws, using materials without permission, or failing to properly cite materials used is illegal and not acceptable.

- Introducing unauthorized or inappropriate self-authored materials for financial gain is a distraction and is not acceptable.

- Unresponsive or unexcused absences from the online workshop/classroom are grounds for immediate dismissal.

Resolving Conflict

The NCPMS Learning Teams shall immediately resolve any conflict that shall arise between participants and/or instructors. The NCPMS Learning Teams shall serve as arbitrators, and all decisions are final.

All participants (NCPMS members or nonmembers) agree to hold harmless the National Coalition of Professional Mystery Shoppers, Inc. (d.b.a. NCPMS, The National Center for Professional Mystery Shoppers & Merchandisers), its organizers, agents, officials, instructors, contractors, and representatives from and against all claims, actions, costs, expenses, and demands.

Learning Center Contact Person

Niccole Rogers is your Online Learning Center contact person if you need any assistance. Niccole can be reached at ncpms@ncpmscenter.org or niccole@ncpmscenter.org. Niccole usually replies to all emails within 24 hours.

Definitions

NCPMS: National Coalition of Professional Mystery Shoppers, Inc., d.b.a. National Center for Professional Mystery Shoppers and Merchandisers.

NCPMS Learning Team: A group of instructors.

NCPMS Online Learning Center: Any online workshop/classroom environment developed or maintained by NCPMS.

Classroom: Any NCPMS online environment that is used for learning.

Workshop: Any NCPMS online environment that is used for learning.

The NCPMS reserves the right to update, change, or add new information to this document at any time without notice. This document was last updated on 02/11/02, 05/27/02, 06/01/02, 07/02/02, 03/04/03, 08/25/03.

CHAPTER

14

KASST TEST
AND STUDY GUIDE

What Is the Knowledge and
Skill Set Test (KASST)?*

The Knowledge and Skill Set Test is a comprehensive exam designed to test and verify knowledge and skill in the following areas. All Contractors taking the test must receive an 87 percent or higher score in order to pass.

Contractor Expertise

- Assignment types
- Payment scales
- Terminology

Conducting Business

- Independent contractors and the IRS
- Ethics and confidentiality
- Declining/canceling/terminating assignments and contracts

- Managing conflict
- Basic math

Advanced Communication

- Writing, spelling, and grammar
- Reading with understanding
- Email etiquette
- Telephone etiquette

Certified Customer Service Evaluator
(CCSE) STUDY GUIDE

About This Study Guide

This study guide was designed to help independent contractors prepare to take the Knowledge and Skill Set Test (KASST). This guide has a strong focus on:

- Business etiquette
- Business math
- Conflict management
- Contract knowledge
- Contract management
- Ethics
- Industry knowledge
- Reading and writing
- Record keeping
- Spelling and grammar
- Technology
- Terminology

Some independent contractors will find this guide extremely helpful, and others may find that it does not meet their needs. For cases where this guide does not meet the participant's needs, links have been provided for additional research.

This is a new study guide. In the event that you locate an error (grammatical, etc.), please make a report by sending an email to niccole@ncpmscenter.org.

About KASST

The National Knowledge and Skill Set Test (KASST) is a test prepared, administered, and managed by the National Center for Professional Mystery Shoppers, Incorporated.

KASST is an exam designed to assess professional knowledge and training in three major areas: contractor expertise, basic business management, and advanced communication.

KASST has 50 to 60 questions. Participants must achieve an overall score of 87 percent or higher.

The first section of the test is focused on contractor expertise and has 10 to 20 questions. The second section of the test is focused on basic business management and has 15 to 30 questions. The third section of the test is focused on advanced communication and has 15 to 25 questions. The participant must not answer more than 3 questions in each section incorrectly.

Each participant will have several opportunities to take KASST. If the test is taken once, and failed, the participant can immediately take the test again. If the test is failed again, the participant must wait 10 calendar days before taking the test again. If the test is failed a third time, the participant will not be eligible to take the test again for 3 calendar months.

Before taking KASST, each participant must register a "secret shopper" profile at http://www.mystshopsol.com. When the profile has been registered, the participant should email Niccole the following information:

- First name
- Last name
- Email address

Taking KASST

KASST is a timed test. It must be completed in 45 minutes or less.

KASST requires the participant to have several tools readily available. These tools are:

1. Three-by-five-card
2. Calculator
3. Pen or pencil
4. Scratch paper
5. Alarm clock

No other tools can be used. Dictionaries, thesaurus, study guides, and so on, are not permissible.

No portion of the test (including the scenario) may be printed or copied.

Getting Certified

Upon passing KASST, the participant will become a Certified Customer Service Evaluator. Certified participants should sign their name as follows:

Niccole, CCSE

Niccole, CCSE (N3-000)

Niccole Rogers, CCSE

Niccole Rogers, CCSE (N3-000)

Certification is discussed in more detail in Chapter 13.

Code of Conduct for CCSEs

1. Cancel or decline all assignments in a timely manner.
2. Perform according to the parameter of each contract.
3. Perform all assignments with integrity.
4. Resolve any disputes in a timely manner.
5. Respect and uphold all confidentiality agreements.
6. Return all emails and telephone calls in a timely manner.
7. Successfully complete all assignments according to the agreed terms.
8. Use mediation as an alternative method for resolving ongoing disputes.

Responsibilities

It is the responsibility of the CCSE to:

- Renew certification.
- Uphold the CCSE code of conduct.
- Respect and support NCPMS policies and procedures.
- Report any harassing or unwelcome behavior to NCPMS.

Resolving Conflict

The NCPMS Learning Teams shall immediately resolve any conflict that shall arise regarding certification.

Participants reserve the right to appeal the decision to the National Conflict Resolution Team (made up of NCPMS members and non-NCPMS members). The National Conflict Resolution Team shall resolve any conflict that shall arise regarding certification. The National Conflict Resolution Team shall serve as arbitrators, and all decisions are final.

Certification Contact Person

Niccole Rogers is the certification contact person if assistance is needed. Niccole can be reached at ncpms@ncpmscenter.org or niccole@ncpms-center.org. Niccole usually replies to all emails within 48 hours.

All participants (NCPMS members and nonmembers) agree to hold harmless the NCPMS, President of NCPMS, Board of Directors, Advisory Board, Volunteers, Associate Contractors, Affiliates, Teams, and Divisions.

The NCPMS reserves the right to update, change, or add new information to this document at any time without notice.

Studying for KASST

You may print this study guide to study. However, it may not be used during the test.

Assignment Types

Audit: An evaluation done to ensure that a product is priced appropriately. Also known as a price audit.

Competitive intelligence: The use of any type of mystery-shopping evaluation on a competing business, firm, or service.

Customer service evaluation: A review of how customers are managed in a business environment. A strong focus builds and maintains relationships with customers. This review looks at the ability to determine customers' needs, requirements, and expectations; value; retention; complaints; ability to determine satisfaction or dissatisfaction; and follow-up.

Integrity evaluation: Theft detection.

Overall performance evaluation: A combination of evaluations to determine the efficiency and effectiveness of customer service management, integrity and theft prevention, product and service availability, and business flow.

Process evaluation: A review of the flow of business, including the ability to handle customer needs, product and service delivery, and the availability and responsiveness of key unit and support services working together. It focuses on alignment of services.

Product and service evaluation: A review of product and service quality, availability, and variety. That includes timeliness and price checks and audits.

Policy compliance evaluation: A review for compliance with applicable laws, and business policies and procedures.

Industry Statistics

The NCPMS (collectively with other firms, groups, and business associates) gathers data from independent contractors to track trends in the industry. A summary of the latest secret shopping (SS) data.

Sex

89 percent women

11 percent men

Age

42 percent are between the ages of 32 and 42

Disability

1 percent reported a disability.

Highest Education Level

28 percent high school

23 percent undergraduate four-year degree

12 percent graduate degree

Race

85 percent Caucasian

8 percent African American

3 percent Hispanic

Vocabulary

Contractors should be thoroughly familiar with the definitions of jargon and industry terms that are frequently used. Review the following list and highlight any items that are not familiar. Contractors can find definitions using the following resources or by visiting www.justshop.org/definition.

www.m-w.com

www.yourdictionary.com

www.onelook.com

www.netlingo.com

www.slangsite.com

1099-MISC

African American descent

Agreement

Allowance

Anonymity

Apparel

Asian American descent

Audio recording

Audit

Bank card

Benchmark

Bid

Blacklist

Bounced check

Breach of contract

Briefing

Business

Business account

Business email

Independent scheduler

Insufficient funds

Integrity evaluation

Internet stalker

Invoice

IRS Form 1040, Schedule C

IRS Form 1040, Schedule C-EZ

IRS Form 1040, Schedule SE

IRS Publication 505

IRS Publication 535

Laptop

Lead

Legally binding

Libel

License

LOIS

Long distance

Main contact

Mediator

Message board

Membership

Mileage

Mobile

Mock shop

Moderator

Monitor

Multiple-choice questionnaire

Mystery shopper

Mystery shopping

Mystery shopping company

Narrative

Negotiate

Newbie

Noncompete

Noticeable

Objective

Objective assessment

Off-site

Online form

Open-ended question

Opinion

Oral

Overall performance evaluation

Overdraft

Overdue

Overhead

Pay advance

Payment

Paypal

Performance audit

Permit

Plagiarism

Policy compliance evaluation

Possession

Precede

Proceed

Process evaluation

Product and service evaluation

Product sampling

Professional

Project

Proposal

Protest

Publication 15A

Questionnaire

Quote

Race

Rate

Rating scale

Recruiter

Reference

Register

Reimburse

Reply

Report

Reschedule

Response time

Restaurant

Retail

Rotation

Rule conformance

Sample

Sample writing
Satisfactory
Scam
Scaling
Schedule
Scheduled C
Scheduler
Seasonal
Seasoned
Self-assign
Self-employment
 loss
Self-employment
 profit
Self-employment tax

Shopper ID
Shoppers remorse
Site evaluation
Slander
Snail mail
Social Security tax
SOHO
SSI
Stop payment
Subject matter expert
Subscription
Suggestive sell
Tabletop shopping
Telephone etiquette

Telephone evaluation
Telephone shop
Terminate contract
Unbiased
Validate
Verbatim
Video shop
Willful misconduct

Canadian Shoppers:
CCRA
T4A
CPP
QPP
T1 General

General Industry Knowledge

Contractors should be thoroughly familiar with general industry knowledge, including but not limited to the following.

Why Businesses Use the Feedback and Comments from Secret Shoppers

1. To determine training effectiveness
2. To gauge employee knowledge and morale
3. To review business procedures and policies
4. To measure organization performance
5. To understand how customers view the business

Characteristics of a Successful Secret Shopper

1. Patient
2. Budgeting skills

3. Comfortable using the internet

4. Excellent time management

5. Detail-oriented

6. Organized

7. Writes well

Forms

1. Multiple-choice forms

2. Narrative forms

3. Rating forms

3. Secret shopping applications

5. Combination forms

Leads

Self-assigned versus per request

Payment Scales

1. Restaurants (free meal to $35)

2. Retail ($12 to $30)

3. Banking/financial institutions ($30 to $70)

State Laws

All secret shoppers should be knowledgeable about Nevada and Florida laws:

Nevada Laws & Statues (Search Private Investigator-Type of Work)
www.leg.state.nv.us/nrs/nrs%2D648.html

Florida Laws & Statues (Search Private Investigator-Type of Work)
www.flsenate.gov

They should also be familiar with applicable private investigative laws in their own state.

Alabama	http://www.legislature.state.al.us/
Alaska	http://w3.legis.state.ak.us/home.htm?
Arizona	http://www.azleg.state.az.us/
Arkansas	http://www.arkleg.state.ar.us/
California	http://www.leginfo.ca.gov/
Colorado	http://www.state.co.us/gov_dir/stateleg.html
Connecticut	http://www.cga.state.ct.us/
Delaware	http://www.legis.state.de.us/Legislature.nsf/? Opendatabase
District of Columbia	http://www.dccouncil.washington.dc.us/
Florida	http://www.leg.state.fl.us/
Georgia	http://www2.state.ga.us/legis/
Hawaii	http://www.capitol.hawaii.gov/
Idaho	http://www2.state.id.us/legislat/legislat.html
Illinois	http://www.legis.state.il.us/
Indiana	http://www.ai.org/legislative/
Iowa	http://www.legis.state.ia.us/
Kansas	http://www.kslegislature.org/
Kentucky	http://www.lrc.state.ky.us/index.htm
Louisiana	http://www.legis.state.la.us/
Maine	http://janus.state.me.us/legis/
Maryland	http://mlis.state.md.us/
Massachusetts	http://www.state.ma.us/legis/
Michigan	http://www.michiganlegislature.org/
Minnesota	http://www.leg.state.mn.us/
Mississippi	http://www.ls.state.ms.us/
Missouri	http://www.moga.state.mo.us/
Montana	http://leg.state.mt.us/css/default.asp
Nebraska	http://www.unicam.state.ne.us/index.htm
Nevada	http://www.leg.state.nv.us/
New Hampshire	http://gencourt.state.nh.us/ie/
New Jersey	http://www.njleg.state.nj.us/

New Mexico	http://legis.state.nm.us/
New York	http://www.nysl.nysed.gov/ils/legislature/ legis.html
North Carolina	http://www.ncga.state.nc.us/homePage.pl
North Dakota	http://www.state.nd.us/lr/
Ohio	http://www.legislature.state.oh.us/search.cfm
Oklahoma	http://www.lsb.state.ok.us/
Oregon	http://www.leg.state.or.us/
Pennsylvania	http://www.legis.state.pa.us/
Rhode Island	http://www.rilin.state.ri.us/
South Carolina	http://www.scstatehouse.net/
South Dakota	http://legis.state.sd.us/index.cfm
Tennessee	http://www.legislature.state.tn.us/sitemap.htm
Texas	http://www.capitol.state.tx.us/
Utah	http://www.le.state.ut.us/
Vermont	http://www.leg.state.vt.us/
Virginia	http://legis.state.va.us/
Washington	http://www.leg.wa.gov/wsladm/default.htm
West Virginia	http://www.legis.state.wv.us/
Wisconsin	http://www.legis.state.wi.us/
Wyoming	http:/ß/legisweb.state.wy.us/

Taxes

Contractors should be thoroughly familiar with the IRS guidelines regarding independent contractors. See www.irs.gov.

Other Helpful Links

Employee vs. IC   http://www.irs.gov/govt/fslg/article/0,,id= 110344,00.html

Form 1099-MISC :http://www.irs.gov/pub/irs-pdf/f1099m03.pdf

Publication 15-A: http://www.irs.gov/pub/irs-pdf/p15a.pdf

Canadian shoppers should also be familiar with Canada Tax Site: http://www.ccra-adrc.gc.ca/menu-e.html

Ethics

Define ethics.

Define business ethics.

Contract Management

Define contract.

Define contract management.

Define legally binding contract.

Be familiar with standard secret shopping contracts.

Business Math

Contractors should be able to demonstrate basic math skills. This includes:

1. Addition
2. Subtraction
3. Multiplication
4. Division
5. Problem solving

A calculator may be used during this portion of the test.

Record Keeping

There are many reasons to keep records. In addition to being used for tax purposes, records can verify payment. Good record keeping should:

- Identify sources of income
- Keep track of expenses
- Keep track of property
- Assist in preparing tax returns

Records should be maintained as follows:

- Bank records (6 years)

- Canceled checks
- Statements
- Deposit slips
- Debt records (6 years)
- Educational records (permanent)
- Employment records (permanent)
- Business records (6 years)
  - Receipts
  - Bills
  - Sales slips
- Income tax records (6 years)
- Insurance policies (while in affect)
- Warranties (life of product)

Fact Versus Opinion

A fact is verifiable. A fact is usually verified using numbers, dates, or policies and procedures. A fact is beyond argument if measuring devices and records are correct.

An opinion is a judgment. An opinion is changeable depending on who is interpreting the evidence or how the evidence is interpreted.

Etiquette

See Chapter 4 or www.emailreplies.com.

KASST Practice Test

The following is a KASST practice test:

1. Mystery shopping began in
   a. 1940.
   b. 1950.
   c. 1960.
   d. 1980.

2. In what type of assignment do you check for theft?
   a. Customer service
   b. Quality control
   c. Auditing
   d. Integrity

3. Who needs mystery-shopping services?
   a. Corporations
   b. Franchises
   c. Individual store owners
   d. Competition
   e. All of the above

4. Which of the following are not a source of contact?
   a. Market research agencies
   b. Mystery-shopping companies
   c. Schedulers
   d. Corporations

5. The only type of assignment in which you may reveal yourself as a shopper is called
   a. Integrity.
   b. Purchase and return.
   c. Quality control.
   d. Customer service.
   e. Product check and rewards.

6. An industry-specific résumé is called
   a. LOIS.
   b. NICKY.
   c. DORA.
   d. ELLEN.

7. Which of the following is not a component of the industry-specific résumé
   a. Introduction
   b. Why you think this type of service is needed
   c. Your best/worst shopping experience
   d. Areas of travel
   e. Demographic information

8. Which of the following are ways to make contact?
   a. Subscribing to message boards

    b. Filling out online applications with market research companies

    c. Asking a local store manager who does the store's mystery shopping

    d. Both a and b

9. Message boards are used for all of the following except
   a. receiving job posts.
   b. communicating a need for assistance.
   c. stating which companies are not paying.
   d. stating industry changes.

10. If you desire an assignment from a message board, you should
    a. hit reply promptly so that you can increase your changes of receiving the assignment.
    b. thoroughly read the posting and reply accordingly.
    c. place a posting stating that the assignment has been filled.

11. It is important not to hit reply to a message posting because
    a. you will be responding to the entire message board, and all the members will see your contact information.
    b. you will receive hate mail.
    c. your personal information may be subject to identity theft.
    d. all of the above.

12. The House Bill HB2444 stated:
    a. It is illegal to mystery-shop without a P.I. license.
    b. All mystery shoppers must currently seek a P.I. license.
    c. It is illegal to complete an integrity assignment without a P.I. license.

13. Why do market research agencies ask for a writing sample?
    a. To test writing skills
    b. To note whether the contractor can report facts only
    c. To note the contractor's opinion
    d. All of the above

14. In order to succeed as a shopper, you must
    a. love to shop.
    b. love to write reports.
    c. love to be around people.
    d. all of the above

15. In order to create a lucrative career as a shopper, you must
    a. make several contacts every day.

b. use your time wisely every day.

c. apply to several hundred companies.

d. all of the above.

16. You can find electronic job postings and leads on
    a. message boards.
    b. leads-only boards.
    c. Yahoo
    d. both a and b.

17. Which of the following is not one of the three ways to view a message board?
    a. Subscribe
    b. Apply
    c. Digest
    d. Physical viewing

18. Which of the following is not the proper way to unsubscribe to a list?
    a. Send a note to the list stating you that wish to be removed.
    b. Send an email to listname-unsubscribe@hostname.com.
    c. Go to the physical web site and remove yourself as a member.
    d. None of the above.

19. An online application might ask for which of the following information?
    a. Race
    b. Annual income
    c. Household pets
    d. Sexuality
    e. All of the above

20. When asked to fill out an on-line application, you should
    a. promptly fill out all the information.
    b. read through the web site.
    c. answer all the desired questions.
    d. call the company and ask how much it pays.

21. Which of the following is the most expensive method for making contact?
    a. Fax
    b. Phone
    c. Mail
    d. Email

22. The most difficult type of report is the
    a. simple yes/no.
    b. full narrative.
    c. rating scale.
    d. combination.

23. The most common type of report is the
    a. simple yes/no.
    b. full narrative.
    c. rating scale.
    d. combination.

24. To be paid for an assignment, you must
    a. visit the assigned location.
    b. turn the report in on time.
    c. get all the required names.
    d. all of the above.

25. What are assignment parameters?
    a. Specific details you must provide
    b. A suggestion of where to go
    c. Helpful hints to utilize
    d. All of the above

26. If you are offered an assignment, you should first
    a. ask how much it pays.
    b. ask what type of report is required and how many pages.
    c. ask for the location and compute the distance.
    d. all of the above.

27. If you are unavailable to complete an assignment, you should
    a. have your spouse complete it for you.
    b. call the location and get names for your paperwork.
    c. call and reschedule.
    d. do the assignment another day.

28. You can submit a report to a company via
    a. the Internet.
    b. email.
    c. the method listed in the parameters.
    d. fax.
    e. all of the above.

29. An independent contractor agreement states all but which of the following?
    a. You must pay your own taxes.
    b. You are covered under workers' compensation.
    c. You may not divulge any information from the assignment.
    d. You cannot open a mystery shopping agency for 2 years.

30. Which of the following is a conflict of interest?
    a. You sister works at the assignment location.
    b. You previously worked at the assignment location.
    c. You are contacted by two companies to complete one assignment.
    d. All of the above.

31. If you are shopping with a small child who is upset, you should
    a. rush through the assignment and hurry home.
    b. call the company to reschedule.
    c. continue posing as an ordinary shopper.
    d. leave the location and process the assignment with the data collected.

32. If you receive an assignment that is not a good match, you should
    a. throw away the paperwork.
    b. call the company and decline the assignment.
    c. write a letter to the company and send the paperwork back.
    d. shred all materials.

33. Assignments are typically distributed
    a. quarterly.
    b. every month.
    c. every day.
    d. every month during the month prior to the assignment.

34. Mystery-shopping companies track contractors' skills with the following method:
    a. Competency tests
    b. Comprehension tests
    c. Rating scales
    d. All of the above

35. When you receive an assignment, what should you not do?
    a. Tell your friends
    b. Look at all the instructions

   c. Note the distance of travel
   d. Review the form

36. *Anonymous* means that
    a. no one should know you were ever there.
    b. you can not tell anyone that you are a shopper.
    c. you should not get caught taking notes.
    d. both b and c.

37. A typical assignment evaluates all but which of the following?
    a. Attitude of the employee
    b. Cost of the products
    c. Organization of the facility
    d. Hazards

38. Quality control means
    a. the presentation of a product.
    b. the stitching on clothes.
    c. prepared to your liking.
    d. all of the above.

39. On your first assignment, it is important to
    a. take notes wherever you can.
    b. bring a friend to help you out.
    c. inspect every area for cleanliness.
    d. leave your assignment under the seat of your car.

40. Which of the following are ways in which shoppers get caught?
    a. Staring at name tags
    b. Stating that you are a mystery shopper, so the associate had better do a good job
    c. Visiting the same location to the point of recognition
    d. All of the above

41. What form is used to establish an EIN in lieu of using your social security number?
    a. SS-7
    b. SS-4
    c. I-9
    d. 1099
    e. W-9

42. Most mystery-shopping companies pay
    a. net 30.

     b. net 60.

     c. net 45.

     d. net 90.

43. What form is used for small business taxes?

     a. SS-4

     b. 1040-A

     c. Schedule C

     d. Schedule S

44. If you net over $600 in 1 year, you must pay

     a. state tax.

     b. federal tax.

     c. social security.

     d. all of the above.

45. If you net over $400 in 1 year, you must pay

     a. state tax.

     b. federal tax.

     c. social security.

     d. all of the above.

46. If you net $200 per year, you must fill out which of the following forms?

     a. Schedule C

     b. Schedule S

     c. Schedule SE

     d. None of the above

47. If you operate at a loss, you must fill out which of the following forms:

     a. Schedule C

     b. Schedule S

     c. Schedule SE

     d. None of the above

48. You worked for a mystery-shopping company and made a gross of $700. What form will the company send you at the end of the year?

     a. 1040

     b. 1090

     c. 1099

     d. 1050

49. What item is not tax deductible:
    a. Telephone
    b. Internet access
    c. Electricity
    d. Mileage

50. Susie received a grocery store assignment that paid a $20 fee plus $5 in reimbursements. The store was 10 miles away at .32 per mile. What is Susie's Net?
    a. $15.00
    b. $14.60
    c. $25.00
    d. None of the above

51. Sally stayed at a hotel that paid $250 in reimbursements only. What is Sally's gross?
    a. $0
    b. $250
    c. $250 minus airfare
    d. None of the above

52. Reimbursements can be classified in which of the following areas?
    a. Other income
    b. Gross
    c. Miscellaneous
    d. Both a and b

53. Reimbursed business expenses should be classified as
    a. other business expenses.
    b. other costs.
    c. legal services.
    d. office expenses.

54. Which of the following is not a method for computing vehicle expense?
    a. Mileage
    b. Travel
    c. Company vehicle
    d. Percentage

55. If you are not sure of a tax item, you should
    a. contact the IRS.
    b. contact an accountant.

    c. guess.

    d. both a and b.

56. An apartment complex assignment typically pays
    a. $10 to $20.
    b. $20 to $30.
    c. $30 to 40.
    d. $15 to 40.

57. A family dinning experience typically pays
    a. $15 plus reimbursement.
    b. $25 plus reimbursement.
    c. reimbursement only.
    d. none of the above.

58. All but which are methods of payment?
    a. Reimbursement only
    b. Barter system
    c. Reimbursement plus a fee
    d. Fee only

59. Which of the following organizations is composed of shoppers for shoppers?
    a. MSPA
    b. NARMS
    c. NCPMS
    d. All of the above

60. Which of the following organizations is composed of Mystery Shopping Companies and services Mystery Shopping Companies:
    a. MSPA
    b. NARMS
    c. NCPMS
    d. All of the above

Identify each sentence below as a fact or an opinion.

61. Dorothy's work was poorly written.
    Fact / Opinion

62. Dorothy submitted all paperwork before the deadline.
    Fact / Opinion

63. Dorothy has 26 incomplete assignments.
    Fact / Opinion

64. Dorothy made inappropriate facial expressions during her interview.
    Fact / Opinion

65. Dorothy submitted an excellent narrative.
    Fact / Opinion

66. Failing to pay an independent contractor on time for work that was correctly completed is inexcusable.
    Fact / Opinion

67. Dorothy won the annual Secret Shopper award.
    Fact / Opinion

Answer Key

1. a	11. d	21. c	31. b	41. b	51. b	61. Opinion
2. d	12. d	22. b	32. b	42. b	52. d	62. Fact
3. e	13. d	23. d	33. d	43. c	53. a	63. Fact
4. d	14. d	24. d	34. d	44. d	54. b	64. Opinion
5. e	15. d	25. a	35. a	45. c	55. d	65. Opinion
6. a	16. d	26. d	36. d	46. a	56. b	66. Opinion
7. e	17. b	27. c	37. b	47. a	57. c	67. Fact
8. d	18. a	28. c	38. d	48. c	58. b	
9. c	19. c	29. b	39. d	49. c	59. c	
10. b	20. b	30. d	40. d	50. b	60. a	

APPENDIX

A

Tax Forms

Form **SS-4**	**Application for Employer Identification Number**	EIN	
(Rev. December 2001)	(For use by employers, corporations, partnerships, trusts, estates, churches, government agencies, Indian tribal entities, certain individuals, and others.)		
Department of the Treasury Internal Revenue Service	▶ See separate instructions for each line. ▶ Keep a copy for your records.	OMB No. 1545-0003	

Type or print clearly.

1   Legal name of entity (or individual) for whom the EIN is being requested

2   Trade name of business (if different from name on line 1)   **3**   Executor, trustee, "care of" name

4a Mailing address (room, apt., suite no. and street, or P.O. box)   **5a** Street address (if different) (Do not enter a P.O. box.)

4b City, state, and ZIP code   **5b** City, state, and ZIP code

6   County and state where principal business is located

7a Name of principal officer, general partner, grantor, owner, or trustor   **7b** SSN, ITIN, or EIN

8a   **Type of entity** (check only one box)
- ☐ Sole proprietor (SSN) _____
- ☐ Partnership
- ☐ Corporation (enter form number to be filed) ▶ _____
- ☐ Personal service corp.
- ☐ Church or church-controlled organization
- ☐ Other nonprofit organization (specify) ▶ _____
- ☐ Other (specify) ▶

- ☐ Estate (SSN of decedent) _____
- ☐ Plan administrator (SSN) _____
- ☐ Trust (SSN of grantor) _____
- ☐ National Guard   ☐ State/local government
- ☐ Farmers' cooperative   ☐ Federal government/military
- ☐ REMIC   ☐ Indian tribal governments/enterprises
- Group Exemption Number (GEN) ▶ _____

8b If a corporation, name the state or foreign country (if applicable) where incorporated   State _____   Foreign country _____

9   **Reason for applying** (check only one box)
- ☐ Started new business (specify type) ▶ _____
- ☐ Hired employees (Check the box and see line 12.)
- ☐ Compliance with IRS withholding regulations
- ☐ Other (specify) ▶

- ☐ Banking purpose (specify purpose) ▶ _____
- ☐ Changed type of organization (specify new type) ▶ _____
- ☐ Purchased going business
- ☐ Created a trust (specify type) ▶ _____
- ☐ Created a pension plan (specify type) ▶ _____

10 Date business started or acquired (month, day, year)   **11** Closing month of accounting year

12 First date wages or annuities were paid or will be paid (month, day, year). **Note:** *If applicant is a withholding agent, enter date income will first be paid to nonresident alien. (month, day, year)* . . . . ▶

13 Highest number of employees expected in the next 12 months. **Note:** *If the applicant does not expect to have any employees during the period, enter "-0-."* . . . . ▶   Agricultural | Household | Other

14 Check **one** box that best describes the principal activity of your business.
- ☐ Construction   ☐ Rental & leasing   ☐ Transportation & warehousing   ☐ Health care & social assistance   ☐ Wholesale-agent/broker
- ☐ Real estate   ☐ Manufacturing   ☐ Finance & insurance   ☐ Accommodation & food service   ☐ Wholesale-other   ☐ Retail
- ☐ Other (specify)

15 Indicate principal line of merchandise sold; specific construction work done; products produced; or services provided.

16a Has the applicant ever applied for an employer identification number for this or any other business? . . . . ☐ **Yes**   ☐ **No**
     Note: *If "Yes," please complete lines 16b and 16c.*

16b If you checked "Yes" on line 16a, give applicant's legal name and trade name shown on prior application if different from line 1 or 2 above.
     Legal name ▶ _____   Trade name ▶

16c Approximate date when, and city and state where, the application was filed. Enter previous employer identification number if known.
     Approximate date when filed (mo., day, year) | City and state where filed | Previous EIN

Third Party Designee	Complete this section only if you want to authorize the named individual to receive the entity's EIN and answer questions about the completion of this form.	
	Designee's name	Designee's telephone number (include area code) ( )
	Address and ZIP code	Designee's fax number (include area code) ( )

Under penalties of perjury, I declare that I have examined this application, and to the best of my knowledge and belief, it is true, correct, and complete.

Applicant's telephone number (include area code) ( )

Name and title (type or print clearly) ▶

Applicant's fax number (include area code) ( )

Signature ▶   Date ▶

For Privacy Act and Paperwork Reduction Act Notice, see separate instructions.   Cat. No. 16055N   Form **SS-4** (Rev. 12-2001)

Do I Need an EIN?

File Form SS-4 if the applicant entity does not already have an EIN but is required to show an EIN on any return, statement, or other document.[1] **See also the separate instructions for each line on Form SS-4.**

IF the applicant...	AND...	THEN...
Started a new business	Does not currently have (nor expect to have) employees	Complete lines 1, 2, 4a–6, 8a, and 9–16c.
Hired (or will hire) employees, including household employees	Does not already have an EIN	Complete lines 1, 2, 4a–6, 7a–b (if applicable), 8a, 8b (if applicable), and 9–16c.
Opened a bank account	Needs an EIN for banking purposes only	Complete lines 1–5b, 7a–b (if applicable), 8a, 9, and 16a–c.
Changed type of organization	Either the legal character of the organization or its ownership changed (e.g., you incorporate a sole proprietorship or form a partnership)[2]	Complete lines 1–16c (as applicable).
Purchased a going business[3]	Does not already have an EIN	Complete lines 1–16c (as applicable).
Created a trust	The trust is other than a grantor trust or an IRA trust[4]	Complete lines 1–16c (as applicable).
Created a pension plan as a plan administrator[5]	Needs an EIN for reporting purposes	Complete lines 1, 2, 4a–6, 8a, 9, and 16a–c.
Is a foreign person needing an EIN to comply with IRS withholding regulations	Needs an EIN to complete a Form W-8 (other than Form W-8ECI), avoid withholding on portfolio assets, or claim tax treaty benefits[6]	Complete lines 1–5b, 7a–b (SSN or ITIN optional), 8a–9, and 16a–c.
Is administering an estate	Needs an EIN to report estate income on Form 1041	Complete lines 1, 3, 4a–b, 8a, 9, and 16a–c.
Is a withholding agent for taxes on non-wage income paid to an alien (i.e., individual, corporation, or partnership, etc.)	Is an agent, broker, fiduciary, manager, tenant, or spouse who is required to file **Form 1042**, Annual Withholding Tax Return for U.S. Source Income of Foreign Persons	Complete lines 1, 2, 3 (if applicable), 4a–5b, 7a–b (if applicable), 8a, 9, and 16a–c.
Is a state or local agency	Serves as a tax reporting agent for public assistance recipients under Rev. Proc. 80-4, 1980-1 C.B. 581[7]	Complete lines 1, 2, 4a–5b, 8a, 9, and 16a–c.
Is a single-member LLC	Needs an EIN to file **Form 8832**, Classification Election, for filing employment tax returns, **or** for state reporting purposes[8]	Complete lines 1–16c (as applicable).
Is an S corporation	Needs an EIN to file **Form 2553**, Election by a Small Business Corporation[9]	Complete lines 1–16c (as applicable).

[1] For example, a sole proprietorship or self-employed farmer who establishes a qualified retirement plan, or is required to file excise, employment, alcohol, tobacco, or firearms returns, must have an EIN. A partnership, corporation, REMIC (real estate mortgage investment conduit), nonprofit organization (church, club, etc.), or farmers' cooperative must use an EIN for any tax-related purpose even if the entity does not have employees.

[2] However, **do not** apply for a new EIN if the existing entity only **(a)** changed its business name, **(b)** elected on Form 8832 to change the way it is taxed (or is covered by the default rules), or **(c)** terminated its partnership status because at least 50% of the total interests in partnership capital and profits were sold or exchanged within a 12-month period. (The EIN of the terminated partnership should continue to be used. See Regulations section 301.6109-1(d)(2)(iii).)

[3] Do not use the EIN of the prior business unless you became the "owner" of a corporation by acquiring its stock.

[4] However, IRA trusts that are required to file Form 990-T, Exempt Organization Business Income Tax Return, must have an EIN.

[5] A plan administrator is the person or group of persons specified as the administrator by the instrument under which the plan is operated.

[6] Entities applying to be a Qualified Intermediary (QI) need a QI-EIN even if they already have an EIN. **See Rev. Proc. 2000-12.**

[7] See also Household employer on page 4. (**Note:** State or local agencies may need an EIN for other reasons, e.g., hired employees.)

[8] Most LLCs **do not** need to file Form 8832. See **Limited liability company (LLC)** on page 4 for details on completing Form SS-4 for an LLC.

[9] An existing corporation that is electing or revoking S corporation status should use its previously-assigned EIN.

SCHEDULE C	**Profit or Loss From Business**	OMB No. 1545-0074
(Form 1040)	(Sole Proprietorship)	**2003**
Department of the Treasury Internal Revenue Service (99)	▶ Partnerships, joint ventures, etc., must file Form 1065 or 1065-B. ▶ Attach to Form 1040 or 1041. ▶ See Instructions for Schedule C (Form 1040).	Attachment Sequence No. **09**

Name of proprietor | Social security number (SSN)

A Principal business or profession, including product or service (see page C-2 of the instructions) | **B** Enter code from pages C-7, 8, & 9
▶

C Business name. If no separate business name, leave blank. | **D** Employer ID number (EIN), if any

E Business address (including suite or room no.) ▶ ....
City, town or post office, state, and ZIP code

F Accounting method: **(1)** ☐ Cash   **(2)** ☐ Accrual   **(3)** ☐ Other (specify) ▶ ....

G Did you "materially participate" in the operation of this business during 2003? If "No," see page C-3 for limit on losses . ☐ Yes ☐ No

H If you started or acquired this business during 2003, check here . . . . ▶ ☐

Part I   Income

1	Gross receipts or sales. **Caution.** If this income was reported to you on Form W-2 and the "Statutory employee" box on that form was checked, see page C-3 and check here . . . . . ▶ ☐	**1**
2	Returns and allowances	**2**
3	Subtract line 2 from line 1	**3**
4	Cost of goods sold (from line 42 on page 2)	**4**
5	**Gross profit.** Subtract line 4 from line 3	**5**
6	Other income, including Federal and state gasoline or fuel tax credit or refund (see page C-3) . . .	**6**
7	**Gross income.** Add lines 5 and 6 . . . . ▶	**7**

Part II   Expenses. Enter expenses for business use of your home **only** on line 30.

8	Advertising	**8**	19 Pension and profit-sharing plans	**19**	
9	Car and truck expenses (see page C-3)	**9**	20 Rent or lease (see page C-5):		
10	Commissions and fees . .	**10**	a Vehicles, machinery, and equipment .	**20a**	
11	Contract labor (see page C-4)	**11**	b Other business property . .	**20b**	
12	Depletion	**12**	21 Repairs and maintenance . .	**21**	
13	Depreciation and section 179 expense deduction (not included in Part III) (see page C-4) . .	**13**	22 Supplies (not included in Part III) .	**22**	
			23 Taxes and licenses	**23**	
14	Employee benefit programs (other than on line 19) . . .	**14**	24 Travel, meals, and entertainment:		
			a Travel	**24a**	
15	Insurance (other than health) .	**15**	b Meals and entertainment		
16	Interest:		c Enter nondeductible amount included on line 24b (see page C-5) .		
a	Mortgage (paid to banks, etc.) .	**16a**	d Subtract line 24c from line 24b	**24d**	
b	Other	**16b**	25 Utilities	**25**	
17	Legal and professional services	**17**	26 Wages (less employment credits) .	**26**	
18	Office expense	**18**	27 Other expenses (from line 48 on page 2)	**27**	

28	**Total expenses** before expenses for business use of home. Add lines 8 through 27 in columns . ▶	**28**
29	Tentative profit (loss). Subtract line 28 from line 7	**29**
30	Expenses for business use of your home. Attach **Form 8829**	**30**
31	**Net profit or (loss).** Subtract line 30 from line 29. • If a profit, enter on **Form 1040, line 12,** and **also** on **Schedule SE, line 2** (statutory employees, see page C-6). Estates and trusts, enter on Form 1041, line 3. • If a loss, you **must** go to line 32.	**31**
32	If you have a loss, check the box that describes your investment in this activity (see page C-6). • If you checked 32a, enter the loss on **Form 1040, line 12,** and **also** on **Schedule SE, line 2** (statutory employees, see page C-6). Estates and trusts, enter on Form 1041, line 3. • If you checked 32b, you **must** attach **Form 6198.**	**32a** ☐ All investment is at risk. **32b** ☐ Some investment is not at risk.

For Paperwork Reduction Act Notice, see Form 1040 instructions.   Cat. No. 11334P   Schedule C (Form 1040) 2003

Schedule C (Form 1040) 2003   Page **2**

Part III   **Cost of Goods Sold** (see page C-6)

33	Method(s) used to value closing inventory:	**a** ☐ Cost	**b** ☐ Lower of cost or market	**c** ☐ Other (attach explanation)

34   Was there any change in determining quantities, costs, or valuations between opening and closing inventory? If
"Yes," attach explanation . . . . ☐ **Yes**   ☐ **No**

35	Inventory at beginning of year. If different from last year's closing inventory, attach explanation . .	35	
36	Purchases less cost of items withdrawn for personal use	36	
37	Cost of labor. Do not include any amounts paid to yourself	37	
38	Materials and supplies	38	
39	Other costs	39	
40	Add lines 35 through 39	40	
41	Inventory at end of year	41	
42	**Cost of goods sold.** Subtract line 41 from line 40. Enter the result here and on page 1, line 4 . .	42	

Part IV   **Information on Your Vehicle.** Complete this part **only** if you are claiming car or truck expenses on line 9 and are not required to file Form 4562 for this business. See the instructions for line 13 on page C-4 to find out if you must file Form 4562.

43   When did you place your vehicle in service for business purposes? (month, day, year) ▶ .... / .... / ....

44   Of the total number of miles you drove your vehicle during 2003, enter the number of miles you used your vehicle for:

a Business .... **b** Commuting .... **c** Other ....

45   Do you (or your spouse) have another vehicle available for personal use? . . . . ☐ **Yes**   ☐ **No**

46   Was your vehicle available for personal use during off-duty hours? . . . . ☐ **Yes**   ☐ **No**

47a   Do you have evidence to support your deduction? . . . . ☐ **Yes**   ☐ **No**

b If "Yes," is the evidence written? . . . . ☐ **Yes**   ☐ **No**

Part V   **Other Expenses.** List below business expenses not included on lines 8–26 or line 30.

48	**Total other expenses.** Enter here and on page 1, line 27	48	

Schedule C (Form 1040) 2003

SCHEDULE C-EZ
(Form 1040)

Department of the Treasury
Internal Revenue Service   (99)

Net Profit From Business
(Sole Proprietorship)

▶ Partnerships, joint ventures, etc., must file Form 1065 or 1065-B.

▶ Attach to Form 1040 or 1041. ▶ See instructions on back.

OMB No. 1545-0074

2003

Attachment
Sequence No. **09A**

Name of proprietor

Social security number (SSN)

Part I   General Information

You May Use Schedule C-EZ Instead of Schedule C Only If You:

- Had business expenses of $2,500 or less.
- Use the cash method of accounting.
- Did not have an inventory at any time during the year.
- Did not have a net loss from your business.
- Had only one business as a sole proprietor.

And You:

- Had no employees during the year.
- Are not required to file **Form 4562**, Depreciation and Amortization, for this business. See the instructions for Schedule C, line 13, on page C-4 to find out if you must file.
- Do not deduct expenses for business use of your home.
- Do not have prior year unallowed passive activity losses from this business.

A Principal business or profession, including product or service

B Enter code from pages C-7, 8, & 9
▶

C Business name. If no separate business name, leave blank.

D Employer ID number (EIN), if any

E Business address (including suite or room no.). Address not required if same as on Form 1040, page 1.

City, town or post office, state, and ZIP code

Part II   Figure Your Net Profit

1 **Gross receipts. Caution.** If this income was reported to you on Form W-2 and the "Statutory employee" box on that form was checked, see **Statutory Employees** in the instructions for Schedule C, line 1, on page C-3 and check here . . . . ▶ ☐ | **1** |

2 **Total expenses** (see instructions). If more than $2,500, you **must** use Schedule C . . . . | **2** |

3 **Net profit.** Subtract line 2 from line 1. If less than zero, you **must** use Schedule C. Enter on **Form 1040, line 12,** and also on **Schedule SE, line 2.** (Statutory employees **do not** report this amount on Schedule SE, line 2. Estates and trusts, enter on Form 1041, line 3.) . . . . . | **3** |

Part III   Information on Your Vehicle. Complete this part **only** if you are claiming car or truck expenses on line 2.

4 When did you place your vehicle in service for business purposes? (month, day, year) ▶ ...... /...... /...... .

5 Of the total number of miles you drove your vehicle during 2003, enter the number of miles you used your vehicle for:

a Business .... **b** Commuting .... **c** Other ....

6 Do you (or your spouse) have another vehicle available for personal use? . . . . ☐ Yes ☐ No

7 Was your vehicle available for personal use during off-duty hours? . . . . ☐ Yes ☐ No

8a Do you have evidence to support your deduction? . . . . ☐ Yes ☐ No

b If "Yes," is the evidence written? . . . . ☐ Yes ☐ No

For Paperwork Reduction Act Notice, see Form 1040 instructions.   Cat. No. 14374D   Schedule C-EZ (Form 1040) 2003

Instructions

You may use Schedule C-EZ instead of Schedule C if you operated a business or practiced a profession as a sole proprietorship and you have met all the requirements listed in Part I of Schedule C-EZ.

Line A

Describe the business or professional activity that provided your principal source of income reported on line 1. Give the general field or activity and the type of product or service.

Line B

Enter the six-digit code that identifies your principal business or professional activity. See pages C-7 through C-9 of the Instructions for Schedule C for the list of codes.

Line D

You need an employer identification number (EIN) only if you had a qualified retirement plan or were required to file an employment, excise, estate, trust, or alcohol, tobacco, and firearms tax return. If you need an EIN, file **Form SS-4,** Application for Employer Identification Number. If you do not have an EIN, leave line D blank. **Do not** enter your SSN.

Line E

Enter your business address. Show a street address instead of a box number. Include the suite or room number, if any.

Line 1

Enter gross receipts from your trade or business. Include amounts you received in your trade or business that were properly shown on **Forms 1099-MISC.** If the total amounts that were reported in box 7 of Forms 1099-MISC are more than the total you are reporting on line 1, attach a statement explaining the difference. You must show all items of taxable income actually or constructively received during the year (in cash, property, or services). Income is constructively received when it is credited to your account or set aside for you to use. Do not offset this amount by any losses.

Line 2

Enter the total amount of all deductible business expenses you actually paid during the year. Examples of these expenses include advertising, car and truck expenses, commissions and fees, insurance, interest, legal and professional services, office expense, rent or lease expenses, repairs and maintenance, supplies, taxes, travel, the allowable percentage of business meals and entertainment, and utilities (including telephone). For details, see the instructions for Schedule C, Parts II and V, on pages C-3 through C-7. If you wish, you may use the optional worksheet below to record your expenses.

    If you claim car or truck expenses, be sure to complete Part III of Schedule C-EZ.

Optional Worksheet for Line 2 (keep a copy for your records)

a Business meals and entertainment	a		
b Enter nondeductible amount included on line **a** (see the instructions for lines 24b and 24c on page C-5)	b		
c Deductible business meals and entertainment. Subtract line **b** from line **a**		c	
d		d	
e		e	
f		f	
g		g	
h		h	
i		i	
j **Total.** Add lines **c** through **i.** Enter here and on line 2		j	

SCHEDULE SE (Form 1040) Department of the Treasury Internal Revenue Service (99)	**Self-Employment Tax** ▶ Attach to Form 1040. ▶ See Instructions for Schedule SE (Form 1040).	OMB No. 1545-0074 2003 Attachment Sequence No. 17
Name of person with **self-employment** income (as shown on Form 1040)		Social security number of person with **self-employment** income ▶

Who Must File Schedule SE

You must file Schedule SE if:

- You had net earnings from self-employment from **other than** church employee income (line 4 of Short Schedule SE or line 4c of Long Schedule SE) of $400 or more **or**
- You had church employee income of $108.28 or more. Income from services you performed as a minister or a member of a religious order **is not** church employee income (see page SE-1).

Note. Even if you had a loss or a small amount of income from self-employment, it may be to your benefit to file Schedule SE and use either "optional method" in Part II of Long Schedule SE (see page SE-3).

Exception. If your only self-employment income was from earnings as a minister, member of a religious order, or Christian Science practitioner **and** you filed Form 4361 and received IRS approval not to be taxed on those earnings, **do not** file Schedule SE. Instead, write "Exempt–Form 4361" on Form 1040, line 55.

May I Use Short Schedule SE or Must I Use Long Schedule SE?

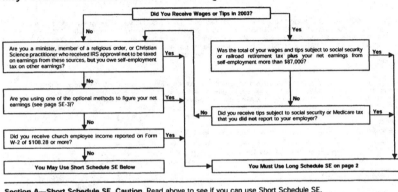

Section A—Short Schedule SE. Caution. Read above to see if you can use Short Schedule SE.

1	Net farm profit or (loss) from Schedule F, line 36, and farm partnerships, Schedule K-1 (Form 1065), line 15a	**1**
2	Net profit or (loss) from Schedule C, line 31; Schedule C-EZ, line 3; Schedule K-1 (Form 1065), line 15a (other than farming); and Schedule K-1 (Form 1065-B), box 9. Ministers and members of religious orders, see page SE-1 for amounts to report on this line. See page SE-2 for other income to report	**2**
3	Combine lines 1 and 2	**3**
4	**Net earnings from self-employment.** Multiply line 3 by 92.35% (.9235). If less than $400, **do not** file this schedule; you do not owe self-employment tax . . . . ▶	**4**
5	**Self-employment tax.** If the amount on line 4 is: • $87,000 or less, multiply line 4 by 15.3% (.153). Enter the result here and on **Form 1040, line 55.** • More than $87,000, multiply line 4 by 2.9% (.029). Then, add $10,788.00 to the result. Enter the total here and on **Form 1040, line 55.**	**5**
6	Deduction for one-half of self-employment tax. Multiply line 5 by 50% (.5). Enter the result here and on **Form 1040, line 28** **6**	

For Paperwork Reduction Act Notice, see Form 1040 instructions. Cat. No. 11358Z Schedule SE (Form 1040) 2003

Schedule SE (Form 1040) 2003   Attachment Sequence No. **17**   Page **2**

Name of person with **self-employment** income (as shown on Form 1040) | Social security number of person with **self-employment** income ▶

Section B—Long Schedule SE

Part I Self-Employment Tax

Note. If your only income subject to self-employment tax is **church employee income**, skip lines 1 through 4b. Enter -0- on line 4c and go to line 5a. Income from services you performed as a minister or a member of a religious order **is not** church employee income. See page SE-1.

A If you are a minister, member of a religious order, or Christian Science practitioner **and** you filed Form 4361, but you had $400 or more of **other** net earnings from self-employment, check here and continue with Part I . . . . . . ▶ ☐

1	Net farm profit or (loss) from Schedule F, line 36, and farm partnerships, Schedule K-1 (Form 1065), line 15a. **Note.** Skip this line if you use the farm optional method (see page SE-4) . .	**1**	
2	Net profit or (loss) from Schedule C, line 31; Schedule C-EZ, line 3; Schedule K-1 (Form 1065), line 15a (other than farming); and Schedule K-1 (Form 1065-B), box 9. Ministers and members of religious orders, see page SE-1 for amounts to report on this line. See page SE-2 for other income to report. **Note.** Skip this line if you use the nonfarm optional method (see page SE-4)	**2**	
3	Combine lines 1 and 2	**3**	
4a	If line 3 is more than zero, multiply line 3 by 92.35% (.9235). Otherwise, enter amount from line 3	**4a**	
b	If you elect one or both of the optional methods, enter the total of lines 15 and 17 here . . .	**4b**	
c	Combine lines 4a and 4b. If less than $400, **do not** file this schedule; you do not owe self-employment tax. **Exception.** If less than $400 and you had **church employee income,** enter -0- and continue ▶	**4c**	
5a	Enter your **church employee income** from Form W-2. See page SE-1 for definition of church employee income. **5a**		
b	Multiply line 5a by 92.35% (.9235). If less than $100, enter -0-	**5b**	
6	**Net earnings from self-employment.** Add lines 4c and 5b	**6**	
7	Maximum amount of combined wages and self-employment earnings subject to social security tax or the 6.2% portion of the 7.65% railroad retirement (tier 1) tax for 2003	**7**	87,000 00
8a	Total social security wages and tips (total of boxes 3 and 7 on Form(s) W-2) and railroad retirement (tier 1) compensation. If $87,000 or more, skip lines 8b through 10, and go to line 11 . . . . **8a**		
b	Unreported tips subject to social security tax (from Form 4137, line 9) **8b**		
c	Add lines 8a and 8b	**8c**	
9	Subtract line 8c from line 7. If zero or less, enter -0- here and on line 10 and go to line 11 . ▶	**9**	
10	Multiply the **smaller** of line 6 or line 9 by 12.4% (.124)	**10**	
11	Multiply line 6 by 2.9% (.029)	**11**	
12	**Self-employment tax.** Add lines 10 and 11. Enter here and on **Form 1040, line 55**	**12**	
13	**Deduction for one-half of self-employment tax.** Multiply line 12 by 50% (.5). Enter the result here and on **Form 1040, line 28** **13**		

Part II Optional Methods To Figure Net Earnings (see page SE-3)

Farm Optional Method. You may use this method **only if:**
• Your gross farm income[1] was not more than $2,400 **or**
• Your net farm profits[2] were less than $1,733.

14	Maximum income for optional methods	**14**	1,600 00
15	Enter the **smaller** of: two-thirds (⅔) of gross farm income[1] (not less than zero) **or** $1,600. Also include this amount on line 4b above	**15**	

Nonfarm Optional Method. You may use this method **only if:**
• Your net nonfarm profits[3] were less than $1,733 and also less than 72.189% of your gross nonfarm income[4] **and**
• You had net earnings from self-employment of at least $400 in 2 of the prior 3 years.
Caution. You may use this method no more than five times.

16	Subtract line 15 from line 14	**16**	
17	Enter the **smaller** of: two-thirds (⅔) of gross nonfarm income[4] (not less than zero) **or** the amount on line 16. Also include this amount on line 4b above	**17**	

[1]From Sch. F, line 11, and Sch. K-1 (Form 1065), line 15b. [3]From Sch. C, line 31; Sch. C-EZ, line 3; Sch. K-1 (Form 1065), line 15a; and Sch. K-1 (Form 1065-B), box 9.
[2]From Sch. F, line 36, and Sch. K-1 (Form 1065), line 15a. [4]From Sch. C, line 7; Sch. C-EZ, line 1; Sch. K-1 (Form 1065), line 15c; and Sch. K-1 (Form 1065-B), box 9.

Schedule SE (Form 1040) 2003

INDEX

ABOUT THE AUTHOR

Ilisha S. Newhouse was born in Brooklyn, New York, and raised in southern California. In 1992, she began to call Arizona home and plans to retire here in the valley. Her education consists of a Licensed Vocational Nurse degree from Brooklyn College at Magna Institute, an Associate of Arts degree in administrative justice from Golden West College, a Bachelor of Arts degree in sociology from Arizona State University, a Master of Arts degree in organizational management from University of Phoenix, and a Doctor of Philosophy degree in theocentric business and ethics from the American College of Theological Studies. Previously, she worked as an accountant, an assistant controller, and a human resource director. She has owned and operated a small market research agency since 1998 and contracts as a consultant to several large corporations. In late 1999, she began mentoring students, and in January 2000, she began teaching courses at the Chandler Community Center. In 2001, she became a community college certified instructor, and she is currently an adjunct instructor in business, sociology, and physical education for South Mountain Community College. She was recently hired as a professor of business by Ottawa University. She is an ordained minister and enjoys performing wedding ceremonies throughout the Phoenix valley as well as offering assistance at multicultural and religious events. In addition, she is on the board of education for the National Center of Professional Mystery Shoppers and is a main proponent of establishing industry certification. The first edition of *Mystery Shopping Made Simple* was used as a textbook and by popular demand was released into the mainstream. Its success was such that a demand for a more comprehensive book was inevitable.